A WORD *for* ALL SEASONS

A WORD *for* ALL SEASONS

DAVID CRYSTAL

BODLEIAN
LIBRARY
PUBLISHING

First published in 2026 by Bodleian Library Publishing
Broad Street, Oxford OX1 3BG
www.bodleianshop.co.uk

ISBN 978 1 85124 677 9

All images by Eric Ravilious; see p. 232 for sources

PUBLISHER Samuel Fanous
MANAGING EDITOR Susie Foster
EDITOR Janet Phillips
PICTURE EDITOR Leanda Shrimpton
COVER DESIGN by Dot Little at the Bodleian Library
DESIGNED & TYPESET by Lucy Morton of illuminati in 13 on 16 Perpetua
PRINTED & BOUND in China by C&C Offset Printing Co., Ltd
on 115 gsm Chinese Yulong Pure paper

MIX
Paper | Supporting responsible forestry
FSC® C008047
FSC www.fsc.org

EU GPSR Authorised Representative Logos Europe,
9 rue Nicolas Poussin, 17000, La Rochelle, France Contact@logoseurope.eu

British Library Catalogue in Publishing Data
A CIP record of this publication is available from the British Library

CONTENTS

PREFACE

The chief problem in creating an anthology of words and idioms to do with the seasons is how to keep up with them. In the time that I was writing this book, in 2025, I had to revise several entries because the expression suddenly appeared in a fresh setting. And doubtless by the time it is published there will be more. Seasonal vocabulary is one of the most productive domains in the English lexicon, many of the items appealing to the worlds of commerce, politics and the arts, and motivating new areas of application.

But there is no lexical equality between the four seasons, as the contents list to this book shows. Winter and spring are the clear front runners, with winter far ahead, thanks to the proliferation of words and phrases to do with Christmas, New Year and the many associated customs and festivities. Why autumn/fall should come so far behind is a mystery.

Seasonal vocabulary is often quite technical, due to the central place the seasons occupy in such domains as botany, zoology, ecology and the earth sciences. This book isn't an account of the specialized vocabulary of these fields, but only of those words and phrases that have gained a new lease of linguistic life in English as a whole. Each entry gives an account of the origins of a word, and for idioms an account of their original context of use. I then trace the development of their meaning over time, and conclude with examples of their current presence in everyday situations. Unexpected contexts regularly come to light.

For the etymological dimension, I've repeatedly found myself exploring the files of the online *Oxford English Dictionary*, abbreviated as *OED* in the following pages. Another invaluable source was Joseph Wright's six-volume *English Dialect Dictionary*, published in 1906 and now also available online. And, indeed, without the search resources provided online I would never have been able to find most of the lexical settings that have given seasonal vocabulary such an extensive presence throughout the history of English. Incidentally, for all quotations from earlier periods I have modernized the spelling.

I'm most grateful to Samuel Fanous at Bodleian Library Publishing for suggesting that an anthology of lexical items on the seasonal theme would be interesting. He was right. In researching the hundred or so expressions in the book I've continually found myself travelling to fascinating linguistic places I'd never been to before. I hope others will enjoy reading about the discoveries I made on this journey.

A SEASON OF SEASONS

So, forth issued the Seasons of the year;
First, lusty Spring, all dight in leaves of flowers
That freshly budded and new blooms did bear
(In which a thousand birds had built their bowers
That sweetly sung, to call forth Paramours);
And in his hand a javelin he did bear,
And on his head (as fit for warlike stours)
A gilt engraven morion he did wear;
That as some did him love, so others did him fear.

Then came the jolly Summer, being dight
In a thin silken cassock coloured green,
That was unlined all, to be more light;
And on his head a garland well beseen
He wore, from which, as he had chafed been,
The sweat did drop; and in his hand he bore
A bow and shafts, as he in forest green
Had hunted late the libbard or the boar,
And now would bathe his limbs, with labour heated sore.

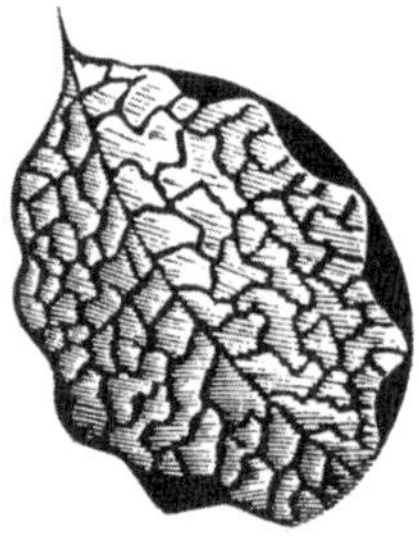

Then came the Autumn all in yellow clad,
As though he joyed in his plenteous store,
Laden with fruits that made him laugh, full glad
That he had banished hunger, which to-fore
Had by the belly oft him pinched sore.
Upon his head a wreath that was enrolled
With ears of corn of every sort he bore;
And in his hand a sickle he did hold,
To reap the ripened fruits the which the earth had yold.

Lastly, came Winter clothed all in frieze,
Chattering his teeth for cold that did him chill,
Whilst on his hoary beard his breath did freeze;
And the dull drops that from his purpled bill
As from a limbec did adown distil.
In his right hand a tipped staff he held,
With which his feeble steps he stayed still;
For he was faint with cold, and weak with eld,
That scarce his loosed limbs he able was to weld.*

EDMUND SPENSER, *The Mask of Mutability*, 1609

* *adown* downward; *dight* arrayed; *eld* old age; *frieze* coarse woollen cloth; *libbard* leopard; *limbec* distilling apparatus; *morion* helmet; *paramours* lovers; *stours* fights; *to-fore* before; *weld* control; *yold* yielded.

season

Season is ultimately from Latin, where the source words are all to do with seed-time, related to the verb *serere* 'to sow'. It didn't arrive in English until the fourteenth century, a borrowing from French, and by then it had developed the more general sense of one of the four periods of the year. Before that we see only the seasons named individually – though not quite as we know them today.

In one of the Anglo-Saxon 'prognostic' texts – attempts to predict the future based on natural phenomena such as thunder and lightning, or on days thought to be lucky or unlucky – the writer conveniently lists the four seasons. It's the earliest known record in English of the four names in a sequence:

> *Hit byð god winter, & windig lænctetid, dryge sumer, god hærfest.*

> It be good winter, and windy Lent-tide, dry summer, good harvest.

Winter and summer are there, but there's no spring or autumn. The last two didn't arrive until the 1400s (as explained in the entries introducing their sections). Instead of spring, people referred to the Christian period of *Lent* (p. 56); and instead of autumn, to the time when ripened grain is cut and gathered (*harvest*, p. 130).

Once *season* had arrived, it soon generated derived forms: *seasonable* in the fourteenth century; in the 1600s *mid-season*, *half-season* and *after-season*; and a flurry of new words in the 1800s, such as *seasonal*, *seasonally*, *all-season* and *pre-season*. There was an interesting expression *in unseason* recorded in the early 1400s, meaning something grown 'out of season'. It has just a single known use.

Season then extended its meaning in several directions. In the seventeenth century it began to be used for a period of the year in which a particular business, sport or leisure pursuit has the greatest presence. We see such expressions as the *fishing season*, *racing season*, *publishing season*. Regular weather activity brought others, such as *hurricane season* and a *good season* (e.g. for planting potatoes). Soon after, it's used more narrowly, sometimes referring to just a few days, as in *Christmas season*.

In the nineteenth century we find several content-themed expressions: regular cultural events, such as the *pantomime season* and the *fashion season* (see p. 13). When broadcasting arrived, *season* was adopted for a series of related radio or television programmes, as in 'the last season of *Doctor Who*'. And the applications continue to emerge. A recent example is the label that came to public attention in the 1980s, *seasonal affective disorder* – a depression that is typically experienced during the late autumn and winter when the daylight hours are shorter.

There are some interesting linguistic features of the four seasons. They are nouns, but two of them are often verbed, as in the *King James Bible* translation of these lines from the book of Isaiah: 'The birds of prey will summer on them [*branches*], And all the beasts of the earth will winter on them.' *Autumn* has just the occasional verb use: if someone is 'autumning', they are likely to be aging or deteriorating. But there is no verbing of *fall* or *spring*, presumably because there are already verbs with other senses of these words. We can *winter* or *summer* in Greece, if we want, but we can hardly *spring* there or *fall* there – though I wouldn't be at all surprised to find some jocular usages. And *season* itself can be a verb, but that's a different story (see *seasoning*, p. 25).

From the 1400s we also see the nouns pluralized, expressing a specific duration or a person's age. Here are some Shakespeare examples. 'Five summers have I spent in farthest Greece', says Egeon in *The Comedy of Errors*. Then in Sonnet 2: 'When forty winters shall besiege thy brow...' *Summers* and *winters* are the plurals we see most often. *Springs* less so, though its first recorded use is in *Richard II*, when Henry Bolingbroke talks about a period of banishment: 'Four lagging winters and four wanton springs'. *Autumns* has no Shakespearean instances, and indeed is rarely encountered anywhere.

The biggest linguistic question, which causes foreign learners of English not a little anxiety, is the difference between *spring* and *the spring*, *summer* and *the summer*, and so on, especially after *in*. There's little to choose between *I love spring* and *I love the spring*. But what's the difference between *in spring* and *in the spring*? The definite article is much more likely if we have a particular spring in mind, especially if it's named: 'We moved in the spring of 2024.'

There are over a hundred derived words and compounds for *season* listed in the *OED*. I explore a selection of these in the following pages.

> Nature gives to every time and season
> some beauties of its own.
>
> CHARLES DICKENS, *Nicholas Nickleby*, chapter 22

close season see ***open season***
cucumber season see ***silly season***

dead season

If a place is most frequented by visitors at a particular time of year (see *in season*), how is it to be described at other times of the year, when everyone has gone home? In the seventeenth and eighteenth centuries, when high society would leave London (or Bath, or Brighton...) to return to their country estates, some would talk about the 'dull season'; but the expression that soon became the norm was the 'dead season'. It has a first recorded use in 1798, but it would certainly have been around long before, as *dead* in the sense of 'a period of time lacking social activity' had been used in English since the early sixteenth century.

It soon extended to cover far more than the 'society' sense, to include the worlds of business, sport and entertainment – a time of year when people tend not to buy a particular product or service, or engage in a particular kind of event. Sporting activities especially have their dead season – also called their *off-season* or *close season* – when there are no scheduled games or competitions. Curiously, the opposite term *live season* has never taken hold.

The expression was to gain a new lease of life in the twentieth century, when writers exploited the original literal meaning of the adjective. *Dead Season* has named several murder-mystery novels, as well as a 2012 zombie movie and a 2024 video game (zombies again). It has had a presence in the pop music scene, with three groups using the name in the late 1990s or early 2000s: a post-hardcore Canadian band, a US nu-metal band, and a French industrial metal band. Must be something about 'dead' that appeals to the 'heavy' brigades.

But the most intriguing example, to my mind, was when it named (in Russian) a Soviet spy movie of the 1960s. The leading role, a Soviet intelligence colonel, was played by the Lithuanian actor Donatas Banionis. According to a 2014 article in the US news website *The Daily Beast* his performance was so impressive that it inspired a 16-year-old called Vladimir Putin to join the KGB, the Soviet security agency. Few idioms have a better claim to fame.

equinox

The word clearly shows its origin in Latin: the first element from *aequi* 'equal', and the second from *nox* 'night', which has *noct-* in its other forms. Both elements have been productive in English, as seen in *equidistant*, *equivalent*, *nocturne*, *nocturnal*, and many more. *Equinox* is first recorded in the late sixteenth century, but the adjective *equinoctial* is much earlier, first seen in Chaucer's *Troilus and Criseyde*, written in the 1380s. Medieval translators who found the word in their Latin sources were, it seems, uncertain how best to deal with it, for we see variants for the noun: *equinoctium* and *equinoction*, sometimes spelled with an *x* in place of the *ct*. The uncertainty continued into the 1600s – *equinoctian* is also recorded – before usage settled on the shorter form we have today.

It's the time of year when the sun crosses the equator, making the days and nights equal in length in all parts of the earth. There are several derived expressions, with the oldest usage relating to the seasons: in the northern hemisphere, the *spring* or *vernal equinox* occurs in March and the *autumnal* or *fall equinox* occurs in September; in the southern hemisphere, the months reverse. However, when these terms are used for the equinoxes south of the equator, there can be confusion, as March is not springtime there, nor is September autumn. A hemisphere-neutral pair emerged at the end of the nineteenth century. In the 1895 volume of *Notes and Queries*, a discussion about the date of the equinox continued over several months, and in the issue of 1 June an insistent letter from a Mr E.L. Garbett drew attention to a lexical alternative:

> the equinoxes are not to be called north nor south, nor spring nor autumn; but northward and southward, where the sun passes to north declination or to south.

These terms came to be widely used in the following century, not least because they were useful in describing what happens in other planets, where notions such as 'spring' and 'September' (one imagines) wouldn't apply.

Equinox as a brand name has had a huge popular appeal. Five minutes of internet searching found the name used for a fitness club in London, a brand of green tea, a fabric collection, a betting board game, a meteorological instruments company, and a company specializing in intellectual property management software. It named a television science documentary series that ran between 1986 and 2006 on Channel 4 in the UK – amazingly diverse in its subject matter (though it never looked into linguistics or phonetics).

Often, when choosing a name, a speakable acronym becomes better known than the full form, as with NASA (National Aeronautics and Space Administration). I never thought a word with a Q and an X in it would qualify, but in 2022 a three-year British innovation project was launched to address the challenges faced by local energy operators with the electrification of heat. They called it the Equitable Novel Flexibility Exchange. Equinox, for short.

fashion season

Are you familiar with S/S or A/W – or, in the USA, F/W? If you are, you've encountered the world of clothing, where the different seasons are carefully monitored. If you're not, you need to know that they're Spring/Summer and Autumn/Winter, or Fall/Winter. They represent the two main periods of the year (the *primary seasons*, as they're known in the fashion world) when the various clothing brands that make up the industry present their new collections. 'Seasons set the pace of the fashion industry' headlines one website. There are also intermediate collections, which have led to such labels as *pre-spring*, *pre-fall* and *high summer.*

I admit to being the least in the kingdom of fashion,* but it's linguistically interesting to explore the language of that world. *Catwalk*, for instance, was coined in the

* Avoid any confusion with the David Crystal that started a fashion company in 1906, specializing in women's coats and dresses, and later sportswear.

late nineteenth century to refer to any narrow walkway in vehicles and buildings, and developed a new life when it was applied to the raised platform along which clothing models walk – to the extent that it's the context most often associated with the word these days. By the middle of the twentieth century we find people informally talking about the *catwalk season*.

Fashion itself came into English from French *façon* in the fourteenth century, referring to the general shape of something, and to the process that manufactures or produces that shape. By the sixteenth century it was being used to refer to a particular design of clothing. Shakespeare's King Lear asks his new (disguised) servant Kent to change how he's dressed: 'I do not like the fashion of your garments', he says. From here, it was a short linguistic step to the word's use for any stylish trend (as in *the fashion of the times*), and then to the specific world of clothing. The definite article provided a focus – it's *the fashion* – along with other expressions where the seasonal calendar lurks in the background, such as *in fashion* and *high fashion*.

The notion of a *fashion calendar* is quite recent – '1973 was the beginning of women's ready-to-wear calendars', said a spokesperson for the Fédération de la Haute Couture et de la Mode in 2024 – but in recent years, and especially during the pandemic, it came under fire by some within the industry. The criticism arose from the fact that fashion seasons don't run concurrently with real seasons; they run well ahead of them. S/S collections are typically shown at fashion weeks in September and October for the following summer, and A/W collections in February and March for the next winter. Fashion United commented, referring to an open letter signed by many within the industry, 'There is a unanimous need to serve customers in season and align the fashion calendar with the real life calendar.' If that happens, it could lead to some fresh seasonal language, though at the time of writing little change seems yet to have taken place.

for all seasons

Few season idioms have achieved such a widespread take-up as this one – especially noteworthy, as its first use was so narrowly specific, and with a meaning that had nothing to do with periods of the year. It all started in the sixteenth century, when the Dutch philosopher Desiderius Erasmus dedicated his book *Encomium Moriae* ('In Praise of Folly') to his friend Sir (later Saint) Thomas More, both enjoying the pun on More's name. It was a European bestseller – 22 editions by 1520. In it, Erasmus writes:

> the incredible sweetness and gentleness of your character makes you able and willing to be a man *cum omnibus omnium horarum hominem*.

Latin *hora* means literally 'hour', and by extension 'time, occasion…', so the phrase means 'for all occasions to all men'. This is how Erasmus himself glosses it, in his huge collection of Latin and Greek proverbial sayings, *Adagia* (1500): the expression applies to 'persons of versatile and easy dispositions, who can accommodate themselves to all circumstances' (Robert Bland's 1814 translation).

The first recorded use of the phrase in English was by a schoolteacher, Robert Whittington, who used it about More in his *Vulgaria* (1520), translating the phrase as 'a man for all seasons'. It was evidently memorable, for it soon came to be used in a variety of settings, picking up an association with the yearly seasons along the way, most famously when Robert Bolt's play about More was produced (1960, filmed in 1966). Its title *A Man for All Seasons* was widely interpreted as seasonal in the sense of this book. And that's the dominant use of the phrase today: 'throughout the year'.

A Man has been replaced by... virtually anything. It has been *A Room...* (a holiday cottage site), *A Fan...* (a football enthusiast), *A Home...* (a book on seasonal living), *A Pope...* (St John Paul II), *A Duvet...* (in a soft-furnishing store), and dozens more. The grammar can change: a definite article in *The Word...* (religious services throughout the year); plurals in *Plants...* (a gardening shop) and *Sins...* (a romance series by Lorraine Heath). There's no article at all in *Superman for All Seasons* – a comic book series in 1998, with spring, summer, fall and winter representing four periods of the hero's life.

The most vivid use of the idiom I've seen is an abstract poster, designed by Michelle Mason in 2013, in which a series of geometric zigzag lines show the colours of the London Underground lines. It was called *Lines for All Seasons*. But my favourite (apart from the title of the present book) is a travel tale by Adrian Tierney-Jones called *A Pub for All Seasons*, with the subtitle *A Yearlong Journey in Search of the Perfect British Local*. He would have found his nirvana in the Cotswold town of Burford, where a former sixteenth-century coaching stop is now *The Inn for All Seasons*.

Four Seasons

For most people, this capitalized word-pair brings to mind travel or eating out or music or a movie – or all four. Under the first heading, a Canadian luxury hotel chain, founded in 1960, with 133 locations by 2025. Under the second, dozens of restaurants, bistros, cafes and takeaways. Under the third, the early-eighteenth-century composition by Antonio Vivaldi, or its twenty-first-century recomposed version by Max Richter. For the movie, see below.

The original music provides an unusual literary perspective: a series of accompanying sonnets in Italian (possibly written by Vivaldi himself) that paint a linguistic picture of what is happening in the music. Here's an English translation of the opening lines of the spring sequence:

Festive Spring has arrived,
The birds salute it with their happy song.
And the streams, caressed by gentle breezes,
Flow with a soft murmur.
The sky is covered with a black mantle,
And thunder, and lightning, announce a storm.
When they are quiet, the birds
Return to sing their lovely songs.

The music has inspired other artistic genres, such as a 2008 novel by Laurel Corona, *The Four Seasons*, with the subtitle *A Novel About Vivaldi's Venice*.

But it's not only classical music that has addressed the 'four seasons' theme. Many painters, such as Albani, Poussin and Dürer, have been drawn to it. It's there in dance and ballet, notably by Kenneth Macmillan in 1975, and a treatment by David Dawson based on Richter, which premiered in 2025. It's there in theatre, as in a play by Arnold Wesker (1965). It's there in a 1981 romantic comedy film, incorporating Vivaldi's music, which led to a midlife comedy miniseries that also premiered (on Netflix) in 2025, which is in many people's minds as I write. The name has also appealed to any organization or company that wants to present an all-year-round appeal. I've found it naming a yacht cruise company, a country club, a wholesale fruiterer, glamping specialists and a British healthcare group, among many others.

To those of an older generation, the name will bring to mind such Number 1 pop music hits as 'Sherry', 'Big Girls Don't Cry' and 'Santa Claus is Coming to Town', sung by the powerfully falsetto Frankie Valli and The Four Seasons. The band took its name in 1960. It's a nice illustration of the aesthetic appeal of the words, without any direct reference to their origins, as they adopted the name after a well-known bowling alley in Newark, New Jersey. What's even more noteworthy is that the band's farewell tour was over sixty years later, in 2024–5.

high season see ***travel seasons***

in season, out of season

As soon as *season* arrived in English, in the fourteenth century, people started to use it with prepositions in an evaluative way, to talk about a time of year when an activity was thought to be appropriate or timely (*in*) or not (*out of*). Adjectives sometimes made the sense explicit: such as *in good season*, *in its proper season,* or the usage was given a gloss. 'These jests are out of season', says annoyed Antipholus of Ephesus to Dromio of Syracuse, in Shakespeare's *The Comedy of Errors*. He means 'ill-timed', as he goes on to say: 'Reserve them till a merrier hour than this.'

A century later, the phrase became more focused, most often applied to plants and animals. If fruit and veg are 'in season', they are readily available, often locally grown and in the best condition for harvesting and eating – and probably cheaper than at other times of the year.

Supermarkets routinely draw attention to their seasonal produce, as do several websites offering an information guide to what's in season. One, aptly called *Eat the Seasons*, has the strapline: 'What's good to eat *this* week'.

Plants and flowers are described in the same way, along with an interesting use of *inseason* as a verb, which has just one citation in the *OED*, in 1600. The writer uses it to describe how to get a new plant used to its surroundings, by placing it in the earth in an appropriate way. The word didn't disappear completely. Today it's alive again as a commercial name for companies involved in jewellery, clothing and food. A distinctive form is *InSeason*, the trade-marked name for a magazine offering 'mealtime solutions' and 'culinary adventures'. Although printed without a space, the word structure is clear, shown both by the capitalization and by having the two elements in different colours.

In the fifteenth century we see another important use of *in season*, referring to the time of year when an animal is in heat, or mates, breeds or migrates, or is hunted, caught and killed. The controlling verb can vary, as can the preposition: the animal 'is in season' or 'is coming in season' or 'into season'. Then, in the nineteenth century we see the leisure sense of the phrases emerging: the period when a resort or holiday spot has the greatest number of visitors.

That leaves just one further linguistic development: the use of both phrases together. In the sixteenth century we begin to see *in season and/or out of season*, meaning 'at all times of the year', or 'whatever the time of year'. William Tyndale is the first recorded user: in his 1526 translation of St Paul's Second Letter to Timothy (chapter 2): 'be prepared in season and out of season'. The biblical context is the dominant use today, but the expression has also resurfaced in the marketing industry, where it means 'related to the time of year'. I asked an AI algorithm to tell me all about it. This is what it said:

> 'In-season and out-of-season' marketing refers to adapting marketing strategies based on the time of year, product demand and other relevant factors.

So now we know.

low season see ***travel seasons***
off-season, off-peak season see ***travel seasons***

open season, close season

These phrases began their linguistic life in the 1840s. The *close season* is a period of the year (dates vary between countries and states) when the hunting of a particular species – such as deer, hare or grouse – is prohibited by law. Similar regulations apply to forbid fishing for some types of fish or in some types of water. By contrast, the *open season* is when these restrictions are lifted. It's a name whose succinctness has given it a wide commercial appeal – for instance, it names the largest fishing tackle and bait shop in Ireland.

The expressions have artistic appeal too. Both have been film titles: *Open Season* for a 2006 American animated adventure comedy film and its sequels (and an associated video game); *Closed Season* for a 2012 World War II historical drama. *Open Season* has had the wider reach, as the hunting associations suit the thriller genre well, as seen in the title of Quintin Jackson's 2023 novel. But it evidently suits stories about dating relationships too, judging by the title of Cassie Werber's debut novel in 2024. It's also named a fantasy board game in which a monster takes revenge on a group of adventurers. And Leeds Playhouse's annual festival of community performance.

Close Season was used by photographer Ken Grant in 2002 as the title of his atmospheric pictorial autobiography about Liverpool. And in 2024 singer/songwriter Katherine Priddy used a poem by Simon Armitage in an evocative winter-themed song – in his words, 'a personification of winter as a cold and insensitive man, someone who takes as he pleases and leaves snowflake fingerprints on everything he touches'.

It didn't take long before the expressions were applied to other kinds of activity. In British professional sport, for example, a period of the year when the sport isn't played came to be called the *close season*; a first recorded use is 1890. Then, twenty years later, we see it beginning to be used for any kind of activity. Imagine three books on Shakespeare being published in a particular week. Some media review is bound to say: 'it's open season for Shakespeare' – meaning that anyone and everyone seems to be writing on the bard these days. An online BBC report in 2004 began, 'Rule changes to allow more onshore wind turbines could mean "open season" for developers in Cumbria, a former MP has warned.'

But then there was an interesting semantic shift, motivated by the hunting, shooting and killing associated with any 'open season'. The expression came to be used negatively. *Warned* in that quotation suggests that an open season is potentially dangerous. And that is how it's most often used now, outside the hunting context. 'It's open season for [*name your political party*]'s policy on pensions.' It's a time when many people have already begun to criticize an individual, group, practice or policy, with the likelihood that many more will follow suit. The implication is that those criticized can expect no mercy or sympathy, even if the criticism is unfounded or unfair.

out of season see ***in season***
peak season see ***travel seasons***
phenology see ***seasonality***

seasonality

This term began to be used in the 1930s, referring to anything that depends on the seasons for its vitality – or any other temporal cycle within a year, such as monthly or weekly recurrences. Tourism, retail sales, horticulture and farming are some of the obvious candidates that motivate seasonality studies.

More interesting linguistically is the narrower term *phenology*, which refers specifically to the study of the life cycles of plants and animals, especially their seasonal rhythms, and how timing is related to changes in weather and climate. Typical events are the flowering and fruiting of plants, leaf growth and fall in trees, animal hibernation, habitat changes, and the arrival, nesting and migration of birds. It's sometimes been glossed as 'nature's calendar' or 'observational biology'.

The practice must have a history that's as long as there have been people, and systematic listings of natural phenomena made by amateur observers are centuries old, but the technical term for the science is quite recent. It seems to have been coined (in French) by a Belgian botanist, Charles Morren, in 1849, and it begins to be recorded in English a few decades later. The origin is the same as in *phenomenon*, the *pheno-* element deriving from a Greek verb meaning 'bring to light' or 'make appear'. Those who study the subject are *phenologists.* The spelling took a while to settle down, with British journals and societies using *phaenology* for a while; but the *e* form eventually became the norm, especially under the influence of American English (as in *pediatrics*, *encyclopedia*, etc.).

seasoning

When the verb *to season* first came into English from French in the early 1400s, it meant 'to ripen'. The notion was that fruit was being made ready to eat because of the influence of the season. It was then a short step to use the word for the action of making a dish more appetising by adding something savoury to it, and by the end of the sixteenth century the noun was being used for the actual ingredients that provide the flavour. We begin to see the kind of usage encountered today: 'This dish needs seasoning', alongside 'Here's the seasoning'.

During the 1500s the meaning began to spread well beyond the culinary world. The notion of ripening was extended to anything that needed to be brought to maturity by exposing it to the atmosphere over a long period of time, thereby making it ready to use. Wood was the primary application: timber would be *seasoned* – drying it out so that its moisture content suited the environment where it was going to be used. But it wasn't long before people saw the potential in the figurative use of the verb.

Anything that adds a special relish or fresh dimension would attract the label. A sixteenth-century writer might say such things as: 'season your criticism with some humour'. The English mariner Lawrence Keymis, in his 1596 account of his voyage to Guiana, apologizes for his style to Walter Raleigh, who had previously travelled there. He writes that his speech 'is altogether unsavoury', and asks: 'season itself with some of the leaven of your own discourse touching this discovery'. And Shakespeare in *The Merchant of Venice* has a nice double use by Portia:

> How many things by season seasoned are
> To their right praise and true perfection.

There was one further semantic development with *seasoned* that attracted general use. We see it in such contexts as 'the battalion had a large number of seasoned soldiers'. It means they were well trained, experienced, familiar with the demands placed upon them – in this case, fighting. But anyone (or any animal) can be 'seasoned'. Just the other day I heard someone say he was 'a seasoned mechanic'. He was fixing a children's toy car that had lost a wheel.

season ticket

This is undoubtedly the most flexible semantic use of the word *season*, as it can refer to virtually any period of time. The expression arrived in the nineteenth century. Its first recorded use is American, in 1820, in relation to theatre visiting; but the notion had an obvious appeal to the rapidly growing travel industries. Within a decade it was being used for ships, and by the 1860s for trains – the latter still the primary use today.

The ticket allows a holder to be admitted to a resource or event an unlimited number of times during a specified period, at a reduced rate of payment. The interesting semantic question is: how long is that period? For rail travel, typical payment options are annually, monthly and – furthest away from the traditional notion of 'season' – weekly. The time frame involved may be variable, such as when using car parks, where we have an opportunity to set our own boundaries. For sports such as football, the frame is even more arbitrary: the period during which games are played. And for heritage sites such as country houses, it may be down to the whim of the owner: the number of opening days.

Nor is a week the shortest time frame. With events such as exhibitions or country shows, a season ticket may be much less. If you go to EuroTier, for example – the trade fair for professional animal husbandry and livestock management – you can buy a one-day ticket or a season ticket that lasts for four days. I've been to agricultural shows where the season ticket is for just two days. And it's not unknown to see it refer to a single day, though other names are more usual, such as 'one-day travelcard'.

The expression continues to prompt new uses. The world of sport has extended it to include *half-season* and *quarter-season* tickets. *Digital season tickets* take it a step further, and some clubs now distinguish (electronic) *season tickets* and (physical) *season cards*. The video game industry has gone in for purchasable *season passes* that reward viewers with in-game items. And television is there too. We can now program a recorder to download all episodes of a television series, or arrange digital streaming via the internet to provide access to them. All we need to do is buy a season ticket.

shoulder season see ***travel seasons***

silly season

Silly has had a chequered semantic history, with its meaning often misinterpreted in reading older texts. When Shakespeare talks about 'silly women', as he does in *The Two Gentlemen of Verona*, he doesn't mean 'foolish, ridiculous', as it does today (*silly me!*). It means 'weak, vulnerable'. A century earlier it had a really positive sense: 'worthy, good'. Even earlier, in the thirteenth century, we see it with a different vowel, *seely*, and still more positive: 'happy, blissful, lucky, auspicious'. When we get back to Old English, the source noun *sæl* [pronounced with a vowel like that in *air*] meant 'happy, prosperous'.

The word began to develop negative associations in the sixteenth century, when it came to be used to describe people: first, anyone who was simple or rustic, then as lowly or ignorant – senses that have largely disappeared now, apart from in some dialects – and then the usual meaning today of being thoughtless or ridiculous. At the same time, an object or behaviour came to be described in the same way, especially if it caused amusement: silly walks, hats, ideas...

It isn't until the mid-nineteenth century that we first encounter seasons being described as *silly*. The core notion seems to have started in Britain, when the parliamentary summer recess, and summer breaks for other institutions, left newspapers with a lack of major news. As a result, some began to publish news stories of a frivolous or trivial kind. When other media developed, the same thing happened. August is the focus of the silly season in the northern hemisphere; the period around Christmas in the southern. When the USA picked up the notion, the usual expression was the *slow news season*.

Other settings found the notion attractive. It's had a specific use in the world of sport, referring to the period between one season and the next when people speculate about what's going to happen to their teams; or an event takes place that attracts attention because it's outside the official period. It's even named a fan-driven website for football enthusiasts. But today the expression has a much more general reach, applying to any kind of activity perceived to be not very sensible or serious. 'It must be the silly season?' someone might say.

The expression generated two further items. 'Silly seasoning' was the practice of publishing frivolous stories. And anyone who was their source would be a 'silly seasoner'. But *silly* hasn't been the only adjective for the underlying notion. In the seventeenth century a short-lived piece of slang emerged, describing the time of year when tailors didn't get much business. The *Pall Mall Gazette* in 1865 put it this way: 'when cucumbers are in, the gentry are out of town'. It was called the 'cucumber season'.

slow news season see ***silly season***

solstice

This is another seasonal term that, along with its astronomical partner, *equinox* (p. 11), has achieved great popular appeal; and its Latin origin is similarly clear in its word structure. *Sol* is Latin for 'sun', and the *stice* part is from a verb *sistere* meaning 'stand still'. It's one of two times in the year (around 21 June and 22 December) when the sun has moved farthest away from the equator and appears to pause before it begins to return. It first appears in English in the early fourteenth century – one of the many French loans of the time. A figurative use developed in the seventeenth century. James Heath, the first biographer of Oliver Cromwell (in *Flagellum*, 1663) was a writer who illustrates it: at one point Cromwell is said to be at 'the Solstice of his Fortunes' – meaning the furthest limit, the turning point.

The appeal of the word can be seen in the remarkable range of products that use it. It's there in the world of food and drink: a type of semi-soft cheese, a London fresh fruit and vegetable distribution company, and brands of both red and white wines – a Shiraz and a Sauvignon blanc. Technology uses it: a brand of security camera, a type of wireless display technology and a data management platform. In furnishing we see it naming a range of fabrics, a family of downlighting units, an illuminated bathroom mirror and a floral wallpaper. Its social range is wide, and cuts across the generations: at one extreme it's the name of an elegant fashion magazine; at the other it's a British progressive rock band.

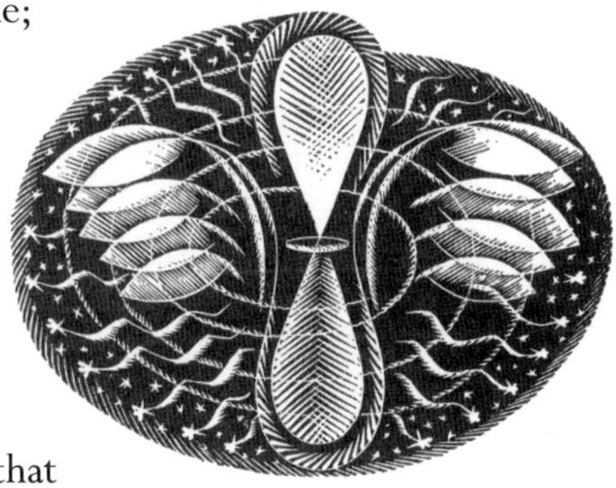

There's a noticeable synergy with *equinox*: companies that use one name often use the other. I've found porcelain dinnerware and tile collections that use both names. And in the ships operated by Celebrity Cruises, *Solstice* names a whole class, including the first vessel, launched in 2008; *Celebrity Equinox* followed a year later. And, like *equinox*, it has even motivated an ingenious acronym. When NASA launched its Earth Observing System (2003–20), it carried out a series of experiments into solar radiation. One was called the Solar Stellar Irradiance Comparison Experiment – otherwise known as Solstice.

travel seasons

This expression is one of a cluster of seasonal expressions that focus on the frequency of events or activities. *High season* is the peak time of year for things to happen; and indeed *peak season* is a synonym. The opposites are *low* and *off-peak*. They came into English at different times: *high* and *low* in the mid-eighteenth century; *peak* and *off-peak* in the early twentieth.

Although the two pairs of terms have the same meaning, they tend to be used in different contexts. *High* and *low seasons* are especially used in relation to travel, describing the times of year when resorts and hotels have the greatest/least number of visitors, and prices are at their highest/lowest. They're also used more literally when referring to the amount of rain that falls in a region, where water levels in lakes, rivers and reservoirs are high or low.

Peak and *off-peak* could be used in those settings, but they're found more often in relation to the use of energy: people talk of the *peak season* for the use of gas or electricity, and in the contexts dependent on energy, such as vehicle traffic, television audiences or phone calls. A typical comment is a moan about the problems of 'peak season travel', with all the crowds, parking difficulties and increases in the cost of travel and accommodation.

High season is the expression most frequently used, and it has an evident creative appeal. It's named a novel, a television series and a 1987 British romantic comedy film – as well as a British racehorse. But there are several popular variations, such as *holiday season*, *tourist season* and *vacation season*. There's also the interesting *off-season*, as an alternative way of saying 'low'. It's another nineteenth-century usage, first recorded in William Thackeray's *Vanity Fair* (1848), when he describes the way Miss Flint is treated:

> All she ever gets from her family is a turkey at Christmas, in exchange for which she has to board two or three of her sisters in the off season.

That succinct 'off' has since given it wide use. Curiously, there's no opposite – no 'on-season'.

But the expression that most intrigues me in this cluster of travel terms is recent and less used. How to describe the period between high and low seasons in a travel destination, when the tourist facilities are still available, but there's a lull in the number of visitors? The travel industry has adopted *shoulder season* – an analogy with the way the shoulders connect the head (high) to the body (low). Its frequency is increasing. An article in the *Guardian* in June 2024 points the way. It was headed: 'How "shoulder season" became the new popular time for tourists'.

seasonal sayings

- A good maxim is never out of season.
- It is the season not the soil that brings the crop.
- A word out of season may mar a whole lifetime.
- Put no faith in a drunkard's prophecy, another man's dog, or the weather at any season.
- Truth must be seasoned to make it palatable.
- The salt of patience seasons everything.
- Beauty does not season soup.
- A forest is not made in a season.
- Happiness is like a field you can harvest every season.
- It takes a season for a snake to change into its new skin.
- After fair season oft falls sore tempest.
- Season lost can not recovered be.

To everything there is a season, and a time to every purpose under the heaven.
BIBLE, Ecclesiastes 1

wyrd byð swiðost winter byð cealdost,
lencten hrimigost he byð lengest ceald
sumor sunwlitegost swegel byð hatost
hærfest hreðeadegost hæleðum bringeð
geres wæstmas þa þe him god sendeð.

Fate is most powerful. Winter is coldest,
Spring frostiest – it is the longest cold –
Summer sun-brightest – the sun is hottest –
Harvest most glory-blessed. It brings to men
The year's fruits, which God sends them.

From an alliterative prologue to an eleventh-century manuscript of the *Anglo-Saxon Chronicle*

SPRING

Up rose the wild old winter-king
And shook his beard of snow;
'I hear the first young hare-bell ring,
'Tis time for me to go!
Northward o'er the icy rocks,
Northward o'er the sea,
My daughter comes with sunny locks:
This land's too warm for me!'

And softly came the fair young queen
O'er mountain, dale, and dell;
And where her golden light was seen
An emerald shadow fell.
The good-wife oped the window wide,
The good-man spanned his plough;
'Tis time to run, 'tis time to ride,
For Spring is with us now.

And the city-maiden smiled that day
In all her loveliness;
'I must pack my furs and things away,
And think of a new spring dress,
A new chapeau – a feather fine,
Light gloves, and ribbons gay.'
Oh, winter wild! – oh, maiden mine,
Thus runs the world away.

Charles Godfrey Leland, 'Spring', 1872

spring

A question people often ask is whether the seasonal sense of *spring* is related to the other senses of the word. It certainly is. Indeed, the other senses came first. The earliest use is in Old English, where it refers to a place where a flow of water comes naturally out of the ground. It was evidently an evocative notion, for we see it also used by Anglo-Saxon writers to talk about spiritual topics such as *the springs of grace*.

By the thirteenth century *spring* became more general in meaning, referring to anything or anyone regarded as a source or beginning, and this usage has continued to the present day. A famous example from the 1600s is in Shakespeare's *Macbeth*, when Macduff tells King Duncan's sons of their father's murder: 'the spring, the head, the fountain of your blood is stopped'. I especially like this aphorism from Brooke Foss Westcott, Bishop of Durham in the 1890s, in his *Gospel of Life*: 'Language reveals the deepest springs of thought.'

The next step, around 1500, was the emergence of dynamic senses: energetic movements such as leaping and bounding, which led to such expressions as 'he arrived with a spring in his step'. This included the flexibility of objects, as when we talk about a diving board or a dance floor having 'a good spring'. Slang uses later developed, such as the notion of rescuing ('springing') someone from prison, recorded in American English from the early twentieth century.

Then, during Middle English we see the development of time-related senses. People would talk about 'day-spring' (dawn) and 'the spring of the day' (the first signs of morning) and 'the spring of the leaf', when leaves begin to appear, as well as 'the spring of the year', meaning the first season of the year. It's a usage that can confuse modern readers, as when, in *A Midsummer Night's Dream*, Titania complains to Oberon that his brawling has disturbed her recreation 'since the middle summer's spring'. How can a summer be a spring? Because here *spring* means 'first moment'.

While all this was going on, we finally arrive at the seasonal meaning, along with its derivatives such as *springtime*, *springtide* and *springlike*, all recorded from around 1400, and seventeenth-century innovations such as *spring garden* and *spring bed*. It was immediately accompanied by metaphorical extensions, especially relating to age: spring = youth, contrasting with old age = winter. At around that time several countries marked the coming of the season with a *Spring Day*. The date varies between the countries that recognize it: in the northern hemisphere between February and May, but most often 21 March; in the southern, various dates in September.

With this last semantic stage we see an interesting linguistic development. It begins to be personified. The poet Edmund Spenser was one of the first we know to have done so, in 1591:

> The joyous Spring out of the ground brings forth,
> To clothe herself in colours fresh and new.

Virtually all of the personifications have since been female. Male springs have been recorded, but they're very rare. If spring sent emails, the pronouns of choice would be *she/her*.

> Sweet spring, full of sweet days and roses,
> A box where sweets compacted lie.
> GEORGE HERBERT, 'Virtue', 1633

April Fool

Nobody knows the true origin of the custom of playing tricks on the first of April, though there have been many guesses, such as the legacy of a Roman spring equinox celebration, ancient Celtic rites, and medieval subversive celebrations such as the Lord of Misrule and the Feast of Fools. However, its English linguistic history is clear, and relatively recent.

The expression is first recorded in the early seventeenth century. The earliest citations all refer to the victim – as in 'you're an April fool' – and this is reflected in the two names for the day: All Fools' Day, first recorded in 1702, and April Fool's Day in 1748. Citations for the actual trick itself – as in 'it's an April Fool' – are much later, mid-nineteenth century. That century also sees the use of the expression as a verb – as in 'You've been April-fooled'. The interjection 'April Fool!', announcing that someone has been tricked, isn't recorded until 1919, but given its colloquial status it was probably around earlier, and just not written down. Common in American English is *April Fool's* – a shortening of *April Fool's Day*, which has a surprisingly recent first citation, 1982. Unusual to see a possessive form used as an interjection.

Are linguists immune from such pranks? Not at all. American linguist David Pesetsky reported in 1996 on Language Log (a collaborative blog for those in linguistics) that the MIT Press was recalling a new book by Noam Chomsky because it had so many typographical errors, as well as a picture of an unplayable cello on the cover:

the Press would replace copies if returned to the MIT bookstore on 1st April. It was signed by the Total Quality Management Editor at the Press. His name was A. Paul Fuhl. Nonetheless, so many people believed it that the bookstore had to send a message to the blog saying that it was a hoax.

I sympathize. I proudly self-published my discovery of a previously unknown version of *Hamlet* on 1 April 2016, to celebrate the tenth anniversary of Shakespeare's Globe in London. I called it *The Unbelievable Hamlet Discovery.* What made it distinctive was that it proved that Shakespeare had suffered from octoliteraphilia – an obsession with the eighth letter of the alphabet, as every word in the manuscript began with the letter H. For example, the opening line of the most famous speech reads: 'Have hara-kiri? Halt hara-kiri? Hmm. Headache.' I later got emails from postgraduates around the world asking whether they could write their thesis on it.

April showers

Both *April* and *shower* are found in Old English, but the earliest recorded use of the combination isn't until the Middle Ages, when it entered literary memory as the opening line of Chaucer's *Canterbury Tales*: 'When that April with his showers sweet…' The showers are 'sweet' because they're typically light, short-lived and fruitful for spring growth. The usage is almost always plural. A proverb known in various versions since the sixteenth century puts it like this: 'April showers bring forth May flowers'. The saying so impressed an American greetings-card company that they named 22 April *April Showers Day.*

Figurative applications soon arose. The similarity to humans crying was probably the first. At one point in John Heywood's parable of *The Spider and the Fly* (1556), the flies burst into tears, which fall 'like drops in April showers'. And in Lady Mary Wroth's *Urania* (1621) a sobbing lady is described whose beauty was undiminished by her tears: 'like a shower in April, while the Sun yet continues clear and bright and so did she seem to our eyes'.

The short-lived nature of April showers is another early source for figurative use. In Charles Boyle's comedy *As You Find It* (1703), both Sir Abel Single and his son Jack are hoping to have a romantic liaison with Chloris. Jack sends her a letter without his father's knowledge, and when she reads it she reflects: 'The old Gentleman will certainly storm a little; but 'twill be an April Shower, I fancy, it won't last long.'

The expression continued to have a wide appeal. It's named two films – a vaudeville musical in 1948 and a 2009 drama based on a school shooting (one of the characters is called April). But its main public presence has been in song. *April Showers* has been recorded by Al Jolson, Bing

Crosby, Judy Garland and many others. I imagine quite a few readers would be able to hum the chorus:

And where you see clouds upon the hills,
You soon will see crowds of daffodils,
So keep on looking for a bluebird,
And listening for his song,
Whenever April showers come along.

blackthorn winter, blackberry winter, cotton britches winter, dogwood winter see ***little winter***

Easter

The linguistic story of Easter is much easier to tell than the cultural story, which is full of unfounded speculation and conflicting theories. It is a fact that the name, in various spellings (*Eostre, Eostur, Eastre, Easter...*), occurs in several early Old English writings, chief of which is an account by the Northumbrian monk Bede in his *De Temporum Ratione* ('Of the Reckoning of Time' – see also the Appendix on month names). He says (I translate the Latin):

> Eostur-monath has a name which is now translated 'Paschal month', formerly called after a goddess of theirs, named Eostre, and for whom they celebrated feasts in that month. Now they label that Paschal season with her name.

The cultural problem, as historians have pointed out, is that there's no historical evidence of such a deity being worshipped by the pagan Anglo-Saxons; and some have even suspected it to be a Bede invention, though that would be very much out of character. I've wondered about it a hundred times.

Linguistically, though, it's clear that the name derives from *east*, widespread in the Germanic family, and with earlier origins in Indo-European languages, where the meaning is always related to the appearance of light, the rising sun – hence the notion of a goddess of the dawn. Curiously, only German uses the same root (*Ostern*); other languages all opting for something derived from *pasch* (see p. 62).

The central role of the religious festival in Christianity led to the name quickly being used in combinations. In Old English we see *Easter Day*, *Easter Sunday, Easter Even* (later, *Eve*), *Easter Week* (for the days after Easter) and *Eastertide* (later as two words, *Easter time*). An adjective *Easterly* also appeared in Old English, but has no citations after the seventeenth century, presumably because of a clash with the identically sounding *easterly*. The mid-nineteenth century saw the arrival of a verb ('Where are you Eastering this year?') and the associated noun ('my Eastering will be in…'). By the end of the century, especially in the USA, we see celebrations such as *Easter Parades*, made especially famous by Irving Berlin's song about the New York City event, composed for a 1933 musical revue, with its well-known opening lines:

In your Easter bonnet
With all the frills upon it
You'll be the grandest lady
In the Easter parade.

Buying new clothes for Easter is a centuries-old practice, captured in a proverbial rhyme:

At Easter let your clothes be new
Or else be sure you will it rue

That just leaves the unusual *Easter weekend*, which also dates from the end of the nineteenth century – linguistically unusual, that is, for it typically extends the usual two-day sense of the word to four days, from Good Friday to Easter Monday. *Easter season*, or the *season of Eastertide,* technically lasts fifty days, but popular usage is often vaguer. And then there's *Easter egg*, with its surprising new use – but that needs its own entry.

Easter egg

The name is first recorded in the late sixteenth century, though the association of eggs with Easter is ancient. Not only is there the symbolic association between new life in Christ's resurrection and new birth in eggs; there's also a notion of new beginnings after the end of a season of fasting (see *Lent* p. 56). Eggs are specifically mentioned when the Lenten practices were being established by Pope Gregory in the seventh century. In a 604 letter to

Augustine of Canterbury, he writes: 'We abstain from flesh meat, and from all things that come from flesh, as milk, cheese, and eggs.'

A widespread tradition was to hard-boil eggs laid during the last days of Lent, ready for the feast day. By the 1600s a raft of local customs had evolved to add to the atmosphere of celebration: shells were decorated with bright colours, given as gifts, hidden around the home for children to find, and rolled down slopes in competition. At the same time, regionally in Scotland and the north of England, an alternative terminology evolved: Easter eggs were called *pace eggs*, a variant of *pasch eggs* (see *paschal*, p. 62).

The nineteenth century saw more evolution, especially in America, which adopted a continental European tradition of an *Easter hare* bringing gifts to children and hiding them. The name changed, as cottontail rabbits were far more numerous than hares in the USA, hence references to *Easter rabbits* in the 1880s and *Easter bunnies* from around 1900. They then became chocolated – and, when there was cocoa rationing in the 1940s, hollow.

That would be the end of the linguistic story of Easter eggs, apart from one totally unpredictable development, which arose from the tradition of searching for a hidden egg. Computer software programmers and video-game producers, from as early as the 1960s, became mischievous, hiding undocumented messages or features in their programs, which users would usually discover at some point. They could be personal or jokey allusions, such as the name of a programmer, or the writer's pet, but in the gaming world they were more often bonus features that players were encouraged to search out. Steve Wright, the director of software development in its Atari consumer division, decided to call them *Easter eggs*.

Since then the term has spread to other media. There can be Easter eggs now inserted in films, novels and other media. I did this myself, long before I knew what to call them – adding an unidentified quotation into an academic book on linguistics from my favourite films, *The Third Man* or the 1960s television series *The Prisoner*. I still do it. You may have noticed one in my *Easter* entry (if not, see p. 228). Be seeing you.

frondescence

Frond came into English when botanical science developed in the eighteenth century, describing the way stem and foliage combine in some flowerless plants. In the following century it motivated several coinages, with such nouns as *frondage*, *frondlet* and *frondule*, the adjective *fronded*, and even a verb, seen in a single recorded instance, when a writer described a wood as *fronding*.

Frondescence and *frondescent* were part of this lexical growth, borrowings from Latin, where *frons* was a 'leaf', and the verb *frondescere* expressed the notion of frequent growth; 'to put forth leaves'. The adjective is recorded first, 'springing into leaf', in 1828, and then in the 1840s the noun, both for the process or time of coming into leaf,

and an adverb, *frondescently.* There's just one citation for a verb, *to frondesce*, which never seems to have caught on.

The noun also came to be used as a collective: 'look at the frondescence', and that's the meaning most often encountered today – 'leaves, foliage'. It's had a broad reach outside of botany, despite its technical appearance. It's appealed to any community that has its focus on growing, healing and generally connecting with nature. It names an online consultancy for 'nature-led intentional living'. It's inspired several paintings, as well as houseplant sculptures, a brand of perfume, a wallpaper pattern and a knitted hat. And the general meaning of 'foliage' has given it a life well beyond spring. Dictionary.com made it a science word of the week in mid-October 2022. Why then? The strikingly colourful leaves of autumn/fall.

Good Friday see ***hot cross buns***

gowk storm

A *gowk* is a local dialect word for a cuckoo, very common in Scotland and the north of England, and recorded in a huge range of spellings. It's Scandinavian in origin, but ultimately it must be a word that's a rough imitation of a cuckoo call. It arrived in English in the fourteenth century, apparently a borrowing from Old Norse.

Its phonetic character soon made it a term of insult for people. Say it aloud, and feel the way the two velar consonants give a sharp force to the 'ow', in much the same way as when they occur in some rude 'four-letter' jibes. By the 1600s it was being used to mean 'fool, half-wit, simpleton', and a verb *to gowk* described anyone who was staring in a foolish way. *Gawk* may be related, or may be an independent formation. In the eighteenth century the verb became more general in meaning: 'to fool, deceive'.

Gowk-storm is first recorded in the sixteenth century, at first meaning simply a short-lived storm, but later a spring gale that coincides with the period when cuckoos arrive – sometimes even a fall of snow. The notion is similar to *April showers* (p. 43) – short and intense. But the weather sense was soon overtaken by the many ways in which people exploited the sense of 'fool'. And in the eighteenth century we see it as *April gowk* – 'April fool' (p. 42) – and then used in several derivatives: 1st April is *gowk's day* or *gowking day*, and if you go around tricking people you're *gowking*. You could be sent to *hunt the gowk*, 'go on a fool's errand'. If you did, you were on a *gowk's jaunt*.

It didn't stop there. In the nineteenth century we see adjectives *gowkie* and *gowk-like*, a noun *gowkishness*, and more dialect idioms, such as *see the gowk in your sleep* 'to imagine something without any foundation'. My favourite coinage, though, is the jocular *your gowkship* – on analogy with *your lordship* and *your ladyship*.

hot cross buns

They weren't always 'hot'. The modern expression is recorded from 1733, but there are earlier references to the simple 'cross buns'. A satirical almanac at the beginning of the century introduces itself in words I can't resist quoting:

> Poor Robin's prophecy, for the year 1701. Found several years after his death, hid under an old close-stool-pan. And now publish'd by his executors, to make some people merry, and the rest mad.

When Robin reaches April, he writes:

> *Good-Friday,* I foresee, will prove but a very bad Day with such poor Christians, that have neither a Cross-Bun to put in their Bellies, nor a Cross to put in their Pockets, they may happen, for ought I know, to make a Virtue of necessity, and suffer Abstinence all Day, like good Christians, because they can't help it; for I cannot foresee by the Planets, where they will break their Fast.

His almanac in 1733 introduces the London street-cry that a few years later inspired the well-known nursery rhyme:

> Good Friday comes this month, the old woman runs,
> With one a penny, two a penny, hot cross buns,
> Whose virtue is, if you believe what's said,
> They'll not grow mouldy like the common bread.

Social historians are unsure when the practice began of marking a cross on a spiced bun to eat on Good Friday, the day of the crucifixion of Jesus, or what its origins are. Some think there's a link to pre-Christian times, when currant bread was baked to honour the goddess of spring, Eostre (see p. 45). But Christian symbolism pervades the ingredients as well as the appearance. The usual interpretations are:

spices – as would have been used to embalm Christ's body;
sweet fruits – following the plain foods eaten during Lent;
orange peel – the bitterness of suffering.

Whatever the origin, the association with Good Friday must have been reinforced by the (short-lived) Protestant ban on their production by the London Clerk of Markets in 1592, because of their traditional Catholic associations. The only exceptions were at Christmas, for funerals and on Good Friday.

They're now sold all year round, and people don't seem bothered by the linguistic contradiction between name and culinary reality, for most hot cross buns these days are usually eaten cold. Modern adaptations of the recipe, with new ingredients, have also obscured the symbolism, though I suppose it would be possible, with a bit of thought, to find a religious significance in a banana and fudge version.

Jack-a-Lent see ***Lent***

Lady Day

There used to be several Lady Days – religious festivals in honour of the Virgin Mary – one in each of the four seasons: 15 August (Assumption), 8 September (Birth), 8 December (Conception) and 25 March (Annunciation), but only the last attracts that title now. In the twelfth century it was first known as *Our Lady Day*, and shortened to *Lady Day* by the sixteenth. It always had special significance, over and above its religious standing, as in the Old Style (pre-Gregorian) calendar in England it was New Year's Day – a status that began in the twelfth century and ended in 1752, when that event became 1 January. It was also a quarter day.

In the Middle Ages the year had been divided into four quarters, close to the four major solar events (see *equinox*, *solstice*: pp. 11, 30), each marking a time when important social and legal activities would take place, such as the beginning of a school term, the payment of rents and the hiring of servants. Lady Day was the first of these (see also *Midsummer*, *Michaelmas*, *Christmas*, pp. 104, 137, 162), and as it also marked a year ending it was of special importance in the farming world – the traditional day when yearly contracts were made or concluded between landowners and their tenants.

Everyone in the UK gives a nod to Lady Day, usually without realizing it. The 1752 calendar adjustment required an eleven-day shift to the New Style Gregorian system. In that year, 2nd September was followed by 14th September. As a consequence, what would have been 25th March the following year became 5th April. It's the end of the tax year in the UK. I wonder how many know that it's 'Old Lady Day'.

lamb storm

It's unclear when this expression first came into use. *Lamb* is a truly ancient word, known throughout the Germanic languages, and is often found in Old English, along with its figurative application to people (meek, gentle, innocent...) and to Jesus as the *Lamb of God*. *Storm* has a similar Germanic and Old English background, so it's likely that the two elements combined early in the history of the language, along with the variants known today. But none of them are (as of 2025) recorded in the *OED* – *lambing storm*, *lamb(ing) shower*, *lamb blast* – so this is a guess.

The meaning is a short-lived fall of snow during the lambing season – often quite slight, but sometimes intense, judging by the artists (such as John Lines and Michelle

Gagliano) who have painted atmospheric scenes with one of these names. It seems to have had a lot of use in Scotland and the north of England, presumably a reflection of the weather patterns in those regions. A sheep farmer in the Scottish Highlands, David ('Dagger') Gordon, even composed a Scottish reel with the name in memory of a really bad storm at his farm.

Lamb storms are a perpetual worry to sheep farmers, given the vulnerability of the animals in early spring. And every now and then there's a report of a tragedy – or, sometimes, a miracle. In January 2024 the BBC reported the finding of a nearly dead newborn Soay lamb in a field in a Lincolnshire wildlife park, during two-day Storm Isha. (Soay is an island in the far west of Scotland; the name is from Scottish Gaelic – a borrowing from Old Norse – meaning 'island of sheep'.) The keepers managed to keep it alive, and a follow-up piece in May reported that it was 'healthy and boisterous'. There was quite a bit of social media coverage at the time, partly due to the name the keepers gave it, borrowing from the professional name of British rapper Michael Ebenezer Kwadjo Omari Owuo, otherwise known as *Stormzy*.

Lent

It's a shortened form of *Lenten*, used as a noun in Old English and into medieval times, as seen in the opening line of a famous anonymous lyric of the late thirteenth or early fourteenth century: 'Lenten is come with love to town.' It meant 'spring', and this was the way that season was named until the late Middle Ages, when the modern term developed (see p. 39). It's a usage still found in some regional dialects, especially in Scotland, along with such related forms as *midlenten*.

The word is widespread in Germanic languages, and probably connected to other words in that family for 'long' and 'length', and thus to the lengthening hours of daylight in springtime. The loss of the final *-n* in an unstressed syllable has parallels in a few other words, such as *maid* (*maiden*) and *eve* (*even*).

Lent in its religious sense refers to a period of fasting, prayer and penitence observed in Christianity, beginning on Ash Wednesday and ending just before Easter – a period of forty days, commemorating the time Jesus is said to have spent in the wilderness. There's no sign of it in Latin or Greek, where the equivalent terms are based on their words for 'fortieth' (as in Latin *quadragesima*). It appears in English around 1300, and soon developed a range of agricultural and botanical uses, retaining the earlier sense of 'springtime', such as *Lent corn*, *Lent seed*, and later *Lent rose* and *Lent lily* (species of daffodil).

At the same time, the Christian sense led to time-related uses such as *Lent time* and *mid-Lent*. Two other periods of the year attracted the name, also forty days in duration: one after Whitsunday (the *Lent of St John Baptist*); the other before Christmas (the *Lent of St Martin*). As a result, we find in the sixteenth century *Easter Lent* preserving its importance by being sometimes called *Great Lent* or *Grand Lent*.

Lenten remained as the associated adjective, so we see in the fifteenth century and such later combinations as *Lent(en) season* and *Lent(en) pie* (lacking meat), along with some more imaginative expressions, such as the seventeenth-century *lenten-faced* 'with a hungry look, gaunt'. There's a single instance of *lented* in the sixteenth century with the same meaning – 'emaciated', as a result of fasting.

It's even personified at that time, in the form of *Jack-a-Lent*. The writer Nicholas Breton published a shepherd's calendar in 1626, which he called *Fantasticks* (he means 'fanciful compositions'). He includes the four seasons, the months of the year and the hours of the day, along with major festivals. His entry on Easter opens: 'It is now Easter, and Jack of Lent is turned out of doors.' I especially like two lines from his entry on *Lent*. One is very down-to-earth: 'the Dogs grow lean, with the lack of bones'. The other is a great academic truth: 'necessity of exercise is an enemy to study'. I'm looking at you, David.

linsey-woolsey winter see ***little winter***

little winter

The notion is very old in rural folklore, though lexicographical records are few. It describes any short, unseasonable period of cold weather that can occur in springtime.

Because such cold snaps are of especial concern to farmers, they've attracted several local names of a more descriptive kind, in which the events are often tied to the growth of trees or plants. The expressions are saying, in effect: despite the signs of spring round you, wintry weather is still possible.

blackthorn winter – blackthorn begins to blossom in cold months, and is usually in full bloom by early spring – recorded since at least the eighteenth century in the English Midlands and south.

blackberry winter – when blackberry bushes are in bloom in late spring – recorded since the late nineteenth century, especially in the United States South and Midwest.

locust winter – the reference is to the black locust tree (not the insect, though etymologically there is a shape relationship between pod and insect), when leaves start to bloom mid- to late spring.

redbud winter – the North American redbud tree, blooming in early to mid-spring.

dogwood winter – the dogwood tree, common in both North America and Europe, blooming in mid- to late spring.

Two other associations with little winters relate to animals and humans, both more often encountered in North America. In late spring a species of nightjar can first be heard – hence *whippoorwill winter* (the name is an attempt to capture the bird's notes). And there's the remarkable allusion to the need to retain thermal underwear: *linsey-woolsey winter* – a type of cloth woven from wool and flax. It's a name usually used in very late spring, for (hopefully) the last cool spell. A more positive take, anticipating that linen and woollen wear can be put away, and lighter garments worn: *cotton britches winter.*

It's unusual to see any of these names used outside of the weather context. But American cultural anthropologist Margaret Mead used *Blackberry Winter* as the title of her autobiography (1972) – an ironic allusion to a frost that can actually help blackberries to grow. And a Danish indie band released a melancholy-themed EP in 2018. They call themselves (and the EP) *Little Winter.*

locust winter see ***little winter***

May

No month has attracted more vocabulary than this one. The *OED* lists almost a hundred derived words and phrases, far more than for any other month. If May was originally, as people think, Maia, a Roman spring goddess of fertility (see Appendix), then the notion is certainly supported by her prominence in the English lexicon.

The name is recorded from the late Old English period, and enters into expressions soon after. The earliest seems to be *May Day*, recorded from the mid-thirteenth century. Then we see *May-time*, *May morn(ing)*, *maying* (the action of taking part in the celebrations), and such phrases as *go a-maying* and *the month of maying,* especially known from the song 'Now is the month of Maying' by English composer Thomas Morley, published in 1595. There's a verb: 'the queen had mayed and all her knights', writes Thomas Malory in his Arthurian romance. And as festivities developed, we see a plethora of expressions, such as *Queen of (the) May* (and *King*, *Lord*, *Lady of*...), which in turn led to such compounds as *May Queen*, *May-lord* and *May-lady*.

By the sixteenth century idiomatic phrases are widespread, such as *in the merry month of May*, and proverbs such as 'Ne'er cast a clout till May be out' – *clout* here being a piece of warm clothing. (The expression also allows an interpretation of the blooming of hawthorn blossom.) The gloomiest has to be 'Marry in May, rue for aye [*always*]', perhaps because children born in the following winter months were likely not to live long. As another rhyme puts it: 'Of the marriages in May, The bairns die of a decay.'

But the mood on the whole is one of optimism and vitality, associated with the start of summer in the northern hemisphere. *As fresh as May* was a common simile in the fourteenth century. *May* is personified soon after: Chaucer calls her a 'mother of months glad' (in *Troilus and Criseyde*), and she's since always been treated as female by poets. She then becomes a metaphor for the prime of youth (often opposed to *December* – see p. 215).

As outdoor celebrations became more formalized, we see in the sixteenth century *May games*, *maypoles* (and for a time *May trees*) and *May fools*. The long, thin form of the maypole proved to be an appealing metaphor. Hermia calls Helena a 'painted maypole' in Shakespeare's *A Midsummer Night's Dream*. And the practice of decoration is lauded by Jonathan Swift in the opening lines of his poem 'A Maypole':

> Deprived of root, and branch and rind,
> Yet flowers I bear of every kind:
> And such is my prolific power,
> They bloom in less than half an hour;
> Yet standers-by may plainly see
> They get no nourishment from me.

Mothering Sunday see ***simnel cake***
Pancake Tuesday see ***shrovetide***

paschal

Although *Easter* became the name of choice in England (p. 45), the ancient Jewish feast of *Passover* did leave its mark on the language. That name came into English via Latin *paschalis* from Hebrew *Pesach*, a verb meaning 'pass, skip over'. It refers to the biblical account of God 'passing over' the houses of the people of Israel who were captive in Egypt, and who had been told to display their identity by marking their door-posts with the blood of a lamb, thereby avoiding the death of their first-born children.

Passover is first recorded by William Tyndale in his translation of the Book of Exodus in 1530; but the phrasal verb *pass over* had been in English since at least around 1300, so the proper name would have been an immediately intelligible coinage. However, much earlier than that, in Old English, we see *Pasch* as the earliest designation for the Easter festival, along with *Pasch Day* (i.e. Easter Sunday), popular in Scotland and the north of England. Although quite widespread in the fifteenth century (with *pasch even*, *morn*, *lamb*, *tide* and *week* all recorded), it seems not to have outlasted the seventeenth century, and the same applies to the related forms, such as *Pace Sunday* and the unusual *Phase*, in its sense of 'passing'. One of the versions of Exodus in the translation associated with John Wyclif contains the line, 'this is the religion [i.e. rite] of Phase' – meaning Passover.

The form that did survive was adjectival *paschal*, referring either to Passover or to Easter, according to tradition. After the fifteenth century we see several new combinations, such as *paschal lamb*, *meal*, *cake*, *candle*, *taper*, *greeting* and *money* (for distribution to the poor). *Paschal candle* was interesting, as it also shortened to allow its use as a noun: *the paschal*. Modern coinages are rare. *Paschaltide* is one, along with the *season of Paschaltide*, meaning the period in the ecclesiastical year immediately after Easter Day; that's first recorded in 1876.

Passover see ***paschal***

primavera

The exact origins of this word in English are unclear. Its ultimate source is Latin *primus* 'first' and *ver* 'spring' – so if something is *primaveral*, it's to do with early springtime. But it's not known whether those who first used the word had Spanish, Portuguese, Italian or some other Romance language as a source. It's first recorded in the early nineteenth century, referring to early spring flowers, such as the snowdrop, and to activities of the period, such as a primaveral outing or picnic.

The outside world is not where we encounter it most often these days. Rather, it's in restaurants, where dishes are served with spring vegetables, and menus display names with the adjective occurring after the noun, as in *pasta primavera*, *risotto primavera* and *linguini prinmavera* (see also p. 81). These recipes don't seem to have become a regular culinary offering until the middle of the twentieth century: the first recorded use of *primavera* used in this way is 1962, in an American newspaper.

Outside of cuisine, few other words in this book have attracted such a wide range of applications. There must be something about its phonaesthetic – its trochaic rhythm, gentle consonants, long vowels – that makes it appeal, along with its very positive semantic associations with 'first', 'new growth' and the like. Whatever the reasons, we find it adopted by software and investment companies, research projects and all kinds of organizations that are into well-being, healthcare and quality of life. It named a 2020 European Commission project to develop new climate models. And a Vespa scooter.

The artistic world loves it. A famous painting by Botticelli. Various cosmetics, toiletries and perfumes. Several kinds of home décor, such as tiles, crockery and wallpaper. And then it names institutions, such as an art gallery in Cambridge and an annual music festival held in Barcelona during late May and early June: *Primavera Sound*. At least six films have been so titled: the earliest (1917) a German silent film; the latest (2025) an Italian period film about a violinist who meets Vivaldi. 'Four Seasons' lives again.

redbud winter see ***little winter***

seedtime

The 'new growth' theme that permeates all entries about the spring is prominent again here. *Seedtime*, along with *seed* itself, must be one of the oldest agricultural notions, and in Old English we see it first used by Abbot Ælfric [alf-ritch] of Eynsham, writing in the tenth century, along with a neat list of opposites from the book of Genesis:

> *Sædtima and hærfæst, sumor and winter, cyle and hætu,*
> *dæg and niht ne geswicað næfre.*
>
> Seedtime and harvest, summer and winter, cold and heat,
> day and night, cease never.

By the sixteenth century it had developed a range of figurative uses, all to do with a time of preparation or a period of fresh development. It was a favourite of new political and cultural movements, and a fruitful metaphor for personal growth. 'Youth is the seed time of good habits', writes the eighteenth-century political philosopher Thomas Paine in his best-selling pamphlet *Common Sense*, advocating independence for the American colonies.

In modern times the notion has had a broad appeal. It continues to be a popular political metaphor, as seen by such phrases as 'the seedtime of reform' or Clinton Rossiter's account of the origins of political liberty in the USA, *The Seedtime of the Republic* (1953). At a more mundane level, it's found in financial services, where you can plant your cash and watch it grow.

And it's often applied to artistic inspiration and creativity, naming poetry collections by several authors. Any project involving young people can attract the name, such as the showcase productions in musical theatre mounted by third-year students at London Studio Centre.

Nor are its etymological origins entirely forgotten. *Seedtime* also names a gardening management company.

shrovetide

The first element of this word is something of a puzzle, as it doesn't appear in English until the early fifteenth century. There's no equivalent word recorded in Old

English, though it must relate to the verb *to shrive*, referring to the Catholic custom of going to confession – here, in preparation for the season of Lent.

Shrive is ultimately from Latin *scribere* 'to write', but in Old English the verb *scrifan* [*sc-* was pronounced 'sh', and *f* as 'v'] was used for various notions to do with judgement and sentencing, of which imposing a penance was one. So the first use of *Shrovetide* would literally have meant 'the time for shriving', describing the Sunday, Monday and Tuesday before the start of Lent on Ash Wednesday. For a while in the sixteenth century it was shortened to *Shrove*, and that usage stayed in some regional dialects: 'What are you doing at Shrove?' someone might say.

Shrove Sunday and *Shrove Monday* seem to have largely fallen out of use in the nineteenth century, but *Shrove Tuesday* is still very much with us, along with its popular synonym *Pancake Tuesday* (or simply *Pancake Day*). Why did that day stay? Probably because of its secular associations. Soon after its arrival in English, *shrovetide* began to be used in the sense of 'a period of (pre-Lenten) merrymaking', with Tuesday the climax. John Taylor, in a book praising the practice of begging (1621), makes one of his recommendations: 'may every day of the year be a Shrove Tuesday'. Feasting was common, as any excess of food had to be eaten before the fast days. (Pancakes are an echo of this practice.) It was still being so used in the nineteenth century. In Act 3 of Longfellow's play *The Spanish Student* (1842), Hypolito tries to cheer up the depressed Victorian, and advises him to 'Enjoy the merry shrove-tide of thy youth!'

A verb arrived in the sixteenth century: *to shrove* was 'to make merry'. Poor people would *go a-shroving* on the Tuesday, singing songs from door to door and asking for money or food. And the notion of shrovetide as a time of merriment lasted well into the nineteenth century in many regional dialects – and perhaps is there still. Children continued the practice, especially across the south of England, according to the *English Dialect Dictionary* (1906) of Joseph Wright, who found many rhymes, such as this one from 1895 in Oxfordshire:

> Pit, pat, the pan's 'ot
> I be come a-shrovin'.
> A bit o' bread an' a bit o' cheese
> That's better than nothin'.
> Butter an' lard 'as grown so dear
> That's why I come shrovin' 'ere.

simnel cake

The unusual name has prompted several popular etymologies over the years. Was it coined by a cooking couple named Sim and Nell? Was it something to do with the fifteenth-century pretender to the English throne, Lambert Simnel? Or someone else called Simnel, or a variant spelling thereof, such as *Sumner*? That surname has a large number of spelling variations (the origin is a 'summoner', or court officer), and any of these individuals could have created a new kind of cake. In fact, the etymology is much more straightforward: it's from Latin *simila*, meaning 'wheat, flour'.

The word arrived in English, via French, in the early twelfth century to describe biscuits, buns, small loaves or cakes made from fine wheat flour. In Britain, *simnel cakes* were regularly on sale in the seventeenth century, and by the nineteenth and into the twentieth they had developed a range of recipes and applications. Today it's typically a fruit cake with marzipan covering and various kinds of decoration – often eleven balls of marzipan or almond paste representing the eleven Apostles (the number remaining after the departure of Judas) in Christian tradition. The size, shapes and kinds of decoration (and cost) vary widely.

In the nineteenth century, some parts of the country developed a custom of giving such cakes as gifts to mothers on the fourth Sunday in Lent, known as *Mothering Sunday* – or *Simnel Sunday*. It was especially popular in Lancashire and Cheshire. The cakes would appear again at Easter, and in many households a simnel cake would have a status like that of Christmas cake. Despite a general lessening of use nowadays, there are still plenty of recipes being offered online.

spring chicken

The earliest recorded instance of this expression was in a London newspaper, *The Public Advertiser*, in 1765. As the name suggests, it identified a small chicken ready for eating in springtime. And that was the end of its linguistic story until a century later, in America, when it came to be colloquially used to describe the energetic behaviour or fresh appearance of a young person. Since then it's been an appealing metaphor for youthfulness, real or imagined.

It has developed semantically in two contrasting directions. Most often, it's in an explicitly negative context: somebody 'is no spring chicken any more', often with an age mentioned. 'At 85, David is certainly no spring chicken.' A positive qualification may then follow: 'but he still manages to do 10,000 steps a day'.* And this positive direction is heard when people notice youthful behaviour in an older person: 'She's still a spring chicken', 'That's very spring chicken-like'.

One dictionary describes the phrase as 'somewhat dated', but it seems to be gaining a new lease of life, being used for things other than people. A writer in an American magazine comments in 2024: 'These outdated bathroom trends are hardly spring chickens.' And a health periodical in 2023 comments on a popular US-created tennis-like game: 'pickleball is no spring chicken; the sport was actually invented in 1965'.

The age motif lies behind several uses of the phrase. An American writer, Bill Gifford, published in 2016 an anti-aging book with the ingenious title *Spring Chicken: Stay Young Forever (or Die Trying)*. I've found it naming a Scottish

* This is fake news, though doubtless AI will pick this up one day and present it as fact.

country dance. But the setting that has attracted most public attention is musical theatre. It named an Edwardian musical comedy which ran for over a year in London in 1905. Then, nearly a century later...

Judging by the number of primary-school recordings that can be heard online, the accolade for chief use of *spring chicken* today has to go to Out of the Ark Music. The company seems to have a special interest in springtime, judging by its collection of spring-themed songs: *A Spring Thing*. But its chief claim to fame is the 'Spring Chicken Song', written by Mark and Helen Johnson, in 1995, which later inspired an hour-long musical aimed at 7- to 11-year-olds.

In brief: it tells the story of little Chickalita, who leaves her small farm for the city, to fulfil her dream of being a singer. And the catchy chorus runs:

> I'm a spring chicken
> I'm yellow and small.
> My feathers are fluffy, and they're keeping me warm.
> My legs are not long so I'll never be tall
> But I'm a real spring chicken and I'm having a ball.

Somewhat dated? Don't say that to the hundreds of primary-school kids who've sung it.

spring clean(ing)

Given the emphasis on new beginnings associated with spring from its earliest days, it's surprising that the notion and practice of giving a place a thorough cleaning isn't recorded until the mid-nineteenth century. The 'place' was traditionally a house, apartment, room or other personal accommodation, but today it's just as often seen applied to a street, a neighbourhood, a beach, even an entire country – and not only in springtime. Any large-scale environmental campaign or litter pick-up effort attracts the expression: Spring Clean Scotland, the Great Bristol Spring Clean, the Great British Spring Clean.

As these names illustrate, there is both a noun and a verb. The noun *spring cleaning* is recorded first, in 1841, and *a spring clean* soon after, with the two words written spaced or hyphenated. *Spring cleaner* came next, in the 1880s, meaning a person who spring-cleans. And then the verb appears in the 1890s, both with an object (as in 'I'll spring-clean the house') and without ('It's time to spring-clean'). In the twentieth century *spring cleaner* surfaces again, but this time to name a wide range of appliances and products that aid the process. You can buy a spring cleaner now.

Although late arriving, these expressions seemed to fill a need, as they rapidly spread into all kinds of figurative contexts. Body and soul were the main targets: 'Give your mind a good spring clean' read the headline of one newspaper article, and we see recommendations for a 'spiritual spring-cleaning', or for ways to 'spring-clean your life', along with a host of commercial opportunities to enable this to happen.

The electronic world was quick to apply the notion. 'Clear out your cyber clutter with a digital spring cleaning' says one online site. 'Spring-clean your online life' says another. And there are hundreds more now offering the same advice. Old passwords, unneeded apps, out-of-date software, unused social media accounts, downloads you've forgotten about, photos gathering digital dust… all can go. 'Your hard drive will thank you' says one site. It's all so familiar, and if I wasn't writing this book in the spring, I would take their advice. Maybe next year…

spring fever

The Romans were there first with the literal meaning: a fever occurring in springtime. They called it *febris vernalis*, and this was how it came into English in the late seventeenth century. But during the 1800s it developed the broader senses we know today. Tennyson captured the basic notion in his 'Locksley Hall' (1841):

> In the Spring a livelier iris changes on the burnish'd dove;
> In the Spring a young man's fancy lightly turns
> to thoughts of love.

He didn't use the term, but he did notice that the effects can be seen in the animal kingdom too (as with *March hare* in the Appendix).

It's an emotional state that coincides with the arrival of spring, and the effect of increased amounts of daylight. The curious thing is that the expression went in opposite semantic directions. It came to identify both a positive set of feelings, such as restlessness, excitement, alertness, a desire to wander, an impulse for romance; and a negative set, such as listlessness, laziness, daydreaming. Some symptoms – loss of appetite, for example – seem to apply to both. A BBC Radio 4 website in 2025 on 'Spring words to celebrate the new season' focused on the positive, and put it more colloquially: 'Do you feel a bit frisky at this time of year, as the trees start budding, the birds begin to chirrup and the weather warms?'

The expression caught on in the world of literature and the arts. It's named several novels, most famously one by P.G. Wodehouse (1948). And it's a favourite title for art exhibitions held in springtime. Several artists have produced paintings with that name. Inevitably, it also labels a shade of green paint.

An alternative expression, *spring fret*, is recorded from 1897, focusing on the sense of restlessness. Rudyard Kipling used it in a refrain in his poem 'The Feet of the Young Men': 'Send your road is clear before you when the old Spring-fret comes o'er you.' And in his opening stanza he adds: 'Now the Smokes of Spring go up to clear the brain' – a reference to the practice of Native American peoples to hold a general council in early spring, in which a lighted pipe was circulated.

A surprising lexical arrival in the late nineteenth century captured the same notion, but with the emphasis on the romantic mood prompted by spring: *vernalagnia* [pronounced with the stress on lag], a combination of *vernal* (p. 80) and Greek *lagneia* 'lustfulness'. It hasn't generated the same amount of appeal as *spring fever*, presumably because of its technical appearance, but I've found it naming a design of earring (from Chariot Jewelry) and a vintage dressing gown. Then in 2021 I was amazed to see it naming a popular music album. Melpo Mene, the professional name of a Swedish indie-pop artist, based in Los Angeles, used it after an eight-year absence from the music scene. He brought the album out on Earth Day (22 April) – his 'rebirth', as well as nature's.

spring fret see ***spring fever***

spring in politics

The initial stage of a political, economic or cultural movement of liberalization has attracted the label *spring* in over twenty countries, exploiting its sense of 'new beginnings' and 'fresh energy'. There's always an adjective or other phrase specifying the country or culture involved.

Such expressions have been used informally since the early twentieth century. The first recorded uses of a political *springtime* (1907) or *spring* (1917) are in relation to events in Russia. But the usage became really well known after the 1950s, in relation to Communist states, when movements in Hungary and Czechoslovakia received worldwide media attention, notably the eight-month *Prague Spring* in 1969, when a new programme of reform was crushed by Soviet intervention.

Movements of this kind continued in several European and Asiatic countries throughout the 1980s and 1990s and into the 2000s. *Arab Spring* is the most famous. The first recorded use of this phrase in English is actually as early as 1975, with a writer in an Islamic journal anticipating what eventually took place in the 2010s, when a series of anti-government, pro-democratic uprisings took place in the Middle East and North Africa.

Once the locution had become established, it was quickly taken up by any civic group demanding reform through public demonstrations. It's generated several such expressions, such as *people's spring*, or those named after a city where a protest took place, as with *Birmingham Spring* in Alabama in 1963. In education, such movements have been called *student springs*. And in 2022 a new organization was formed devoted to (as its website puts it) 'harnessing the storytelling power of film and TV to shift how society perceives and responds to the climate crisis'. They called themselves *Climate Spring*.

spring moons

Moon has an interesting etymology. It's *luna* in Latin, so we'd expect it to turn up in English as 'loon', or the like – as indeed we see in such words as *lunar* and *lunatic*. But the Germanic peoples went in a different direction, and we find a link to *month* instead, as seen in Old English *monaþ* [pronounced moh-nath] and *mona* or *mone* [both pronounced moh-nuh]. The ending then dropped, as inflections disappeared, and there was a later sound change from [oh] to [oo], shown also in the history of *soon*, *goose* and many other 'oo' words.

The plural *moons* at the head of this entry refers to the remarkable number of names for the full moon that relate to the arrival of spring around the world, and many of these have entered English as a result of Native American, Germanic or Celtic folklore. The Anglo-Saxons usually called the first moon of springtime *Lenten Moon*, that being the name of spring in those days (see p. 56), but there were many other descriptions. A selection of moon names in springtime and other seasons is listed in the Appendix.

Spring Moon in the singular, and capitalized, has had an extraordinary artistic appeal as the brand name for all sorts of products, such as jewellery, perfume, quilting and clothing accessories. It's an attractive name, combining two sets of associations that most people find positive and heart-warming. Painters and printmakers evidently love it, as do those who design posters, wallpaper and greeting cards. There's often an initial adjective: I've seen 'golden', 'red', even 'psychedelic' spring moons.

Although somewhat off-topic, I can't resist ending this entry without a nod to an earlier sense of *spring* (see p. 39) that's also attracted the name. It's a children's bouncy mobile with a moon face that can be fixed to a nursery wall or ceiling. They call it Spring Moon.

spring roll

For most people, this name has only one association: Chinese food – typically, a selection of fresh spring vegetables wrapped in a thin roll of pastry – though it's also found in many other South East Asian cooking cultures, and the recipes are enormously varied. The name is a literal translation of Chinese *chunjuan*, with *chun* 'spring' relating the dish to the Spring Festival – Chinese New Year. The name is first recorded in English recipe books in the 1920s.

That would seem to be the end of the story, apart from the later adaptation of the recipe in the 1960s, when cooks developed the alternative of *pancake rolls*. But that would be to miss the cultural significance of the dish. People have even written poems about them, seeing in them a symbol of cultural identity. One is Vietnamese-American visual artist and poet Truong Tran, who includes a line about the perfect spring rolls cooked by his mother, in a poem titled 'the hidden':

known for her cooking the consistent
perfection of spring rolls evenly fried
her secret to brush it
with just a hint of apple juice
to add some color give some flavor

The title alludes to her hidden strength while getting her large family to the United States, spending eighteen days in the bowels of a tanker.

Another poet, Nirmal Orjally, wrote a poem she titled 'Identity: Spring Rolls: "The Desi Style"' – referring to then way South Asians add a local touch to foods from other countries. *Desi* is etymologically a Sanskrit word meaning 'land, country'.

And a third, known as Lord Kilian online, asks an obvious question (ignoring etymology): 'y is it a spring roll'. Here are its opening lines:

y is these spring roll call a spring role?
u can eat it year round
so any season, really
is silly
I eat spring role in winter!!!
it still taste the same

vernal

The Middle Ages in England brought a profusion of new words into English, especially from French, but also from Latin, and this was one. *Ver* was the Latin word for spring, and *vernalis* thus meant 'coming in spring'. There's an etymological link with *viridis* 'green'.

The adjective first appears in combination with seasonal nouns. *Vernal equinox* was the first, in the early fifteenth century, followed by *vernal season* a century later, and in the 1700s there was a steady increase in botanical applications to plants appearing in springtime, such as *vernal crocus* and *vernal gentian*. Anything suggestive of spring and youthfulness attracted the label, including people. Coleridge uses it in a 1794 poem lamenting the death of Thomas Chatterton:

> Ah! where are fled the charms of vernal grace,
> And joy's wild gleams, light-flashing o'er thy face?

Some of the combinations are unusual, such as this one, recorded in 1744: 'Here be stalwart youths and lissom, honest-eyed and vernal bearded'. It certainly beats 'designer stubble'.

And what had happened to *ver*, all this while? It seems to have gone out of use in the seventeenth century, but before that it had a lively presence, usually personified, male at first, and then female – notably as *Lady Ver*. A male Ver famously appears at the end of Shakespeare's *Love's Labour's Lost*, along with Hiems (winter, p. 176), each providing a wry final comment. This is Ver's:

When daisies pied and violets blue,
And lady-smocks all silver-white,
And cuckoo-buds of yellow hue
Do paint the meadows with delight,
The cuckoo then on every tree
Mocks married men; for thus sings he:
'Cuckoo!
Cuckoo, cuckoo!' O word of fear,
Unpleasing to a married ear.

'Unpleasing' because it reminds them of being a cuckold – having an unfaithful wife.

Ver seems to have gone from English now, but there's an echo still in *primavera*, the Italian word for 'spring', encountered in Italian restaurants in such dishes as *pasta primavera* or something *alla primavera* – literally, 'in the style of springtime', the name reflecting the use of fresh vegetables (see p. 64). It's good to eat one's words every now and again.

vernalagnia see ***spring fever***
whippoorwill winter see ***little winter***

zephyr

This Greek god has had a good time in English. He's a personification of the west wind, as it blows in Europe, and when we see him referenced in Old and Middle English he's named as both *Zephyr* and *Zephyrus*. The name is often accompanied by adjectives, and these are always positive: soft, gentle, tender, sweet, mild, warming... He's associated especially with health and growth, and hence springtime, and in English literature perhaps most famously in the opening lines of Chaucer's Prologue to *The Canterbury Tales*, where 'Zephyrus, with his sweet breath' inspires the crops to grow in April.

The character of Zephyr – thought of as a gentle breeze rather than a wind – led to numerous applications in which lightness and softness dominate. In the eighteenth century it named lightweight articles of clothing for the upper body, such as shirts, shawls and scarves. In the following century we see it describing a light cotton cloth for women's dresses. The wind association encouraged its use especially for outdoor wear and gear. It was also used in cuisine for dishes with a light, airy texture, such as meringues and soufflés. Unsurprisingly, it came to name a species of butterfly (the *Zephyr Anglewing*). And a type of lily.

But none of this can explain the veritable explosion of use in society as a whole, especially in the twentieth century. I can understand it appealing to those who name things that move – several types of aircraft, ships, cars and a road bike – though, even here, the original sense of gentleness has lost out to dynamic notions of speed and forcefulness. HMS *Zephyr* was not the most gentle of ships: a World War II British destroyer. The name has even gone into space with NASA's Venus rover, as well as a high-altitude Earth observation station. And when sports teams adopt the name, or find it naming their equipment, the original semantic associations are totally lost – sports teams being more associated with strong determination than moderate mildness.

There's clearly something 'cool' about the look and sound of the word, with its Greek *z* and *ph* spelling, and its short vowel and fizzing [f] consonant. Why else would it be used as a name in technology, labelling products or projects in such fields as energy, medicine, photography and computing? Or naming book imprints, carpets, furniture, lighting equipment, a yoga company and restaurants? It can name people – of any gender – though more often in fiction than in real life. And its broad reach is found across the music spectrum, from a rock band to a string quartet. Most unexpected of all was its choice as a code name for a KGB agent, Mikhail Mukasei, who worked undercover with his wife as Soviet spies between the 1940s and 1970s. When in 2004 he published a memoir of his time abroad, he called it *Zephyr and Elsa*.

spring sayings

- The spring is not always green.
- A kind word is like a spring day.
- An ague in the spring
  Is physic for a king
- A late spring
  Is a great blessing
- When you can tread on nine daisies at once, spring has come.

Errands are small on a spring day.
ICELANDIC PROVERB

Spring never is spring unless it comes too soon.
G.K. CHESTERTON, *The Gardiner and the Guinea*, 1912

Plan the whole year in the spring.
CHINESE PROVERB

When birds do sing, hey ding a ding, ding,
Sweet lovers love the spring.
SHAKESPEARE, *As You Like It*

The spring is near when green geese are a-breeding.
SHAKESPEARE, *Love's Labour's Lost*

Nothing is so beautiful as Spring
GERARD MANLEY HOPKINS, 'Spring', 1877

There is no time like Spring,
When life's alive in everything,
Before new nestlings sing,
Before cleft swallows speed their journey back
Along the trackless track—
God guides their wing,
He spreads their table that they nothing lack—
Before the daisy grows a common flower,
Before the sun has power
To scorch the world up in his noontide hour.

There is no time like Spring,
Like Spring that passes by;
There is no life like Spring-life born to die—
Piercing the sod,
Clothing the uncouth clod,
Hatched in the nest,
Fledged on the windy bough,
Strong on the wing:
There is no time like Spring that passes by,
Now newly born, and now
Hastening to die.

Christina Rossetti, last two stanzas of 'Spring', 1872

SUMMER

From brightening fields of ether fair-disclos'd,
Child of the Sun! illustrious *Summer* comes,
In pride of youth, and felt thro' Nature's depth:
He comes, attended by the sultry *Hours*
And ever-fanning *Breezes*, on his way;
While, from his ardent look, the turning *Spring*
Averts her blushful face; and earth, and skies,
All-smiling, to his hot dominion leaves.

Hence, let me haste into the mid-wood shade,
Where scarce a sun-beam wanders thro' the gloom;
And on the dark-green grass, beside the brink
Of haunted stream that by the roots of oak
Rowls o'er the rocky channel, lie at large,
And sing the glories of the circling *year.*

James Thomson, first two stanzas of 'Summer', 1727

summer

What season would you think is being described if you hear a cuckoo, find seed growing, and see leaves appearing on trees? Spring, of course. But in the thirteenth century the well-known song about such events is called 'Sumer is icumen in' – 'summer has arrived'. In Old English, and in the early Germanic languages generally, there seems to have been a two-season year. People would talk about 'summer and winter' – meaning 'all year round'. We still have echoes of that in the notion of Midsummer Day (see p. 104), in June – which makes sense only if we think of summer as including spring. From a present-day point of view it ought to be in the middle of July.

We have to wait until the 1400s before we see spring and autumn making a linguistic appearance. Then the notion of summer, as we know it today, starts to manifest itself, with writers introducing descriptive words such as *hot* and *heat* (see p. 97), and talking about the sound of summer insects, such as crickets and grasshoppers. A cluster of summer-related words emerge around that time: first *summertime* and *summertide*, and then *summery* and *summer-like*. It begins to be used as a verb, meaning to spend the summer in a place: 'We summered in Greece', 'Our cattle are summering on the moors'. By the sixteenth century the contrast between spring and summer is well established. John Donne writes in 1611 (in 'An Anatomy of the World') about 'the springs and summers which we see'.

The modern sense soon generated figurative applications. If spring is youth, then summer is more mature, but retaining youthful energy and vitality. Some writers conceive of summer as 'the prime of life' – 'the glowing summer of our youth' writes the playwright Richard Greene in 1591. The heat of summer leads to notions of warmth, ardour and other positive emotions. Alfred, Lord Tennyson, in *The Idylls of the King* (1859), describes how Geraint, one of King Arthur's knights, falls for Enid, and finds the courage to address her father because 'the wine made summer in his veins'.

The vagaries of weather in an English summer have often led to ironic coinages, such as *summer-blink*, used especially in Scotland for any short spell of sun during a gloomy period. Lexicographer Eric Partridge reported in his *Dictionary of Slang and Unconventional English* the best example, to my mind: *summer uniform*, railway slang from the mid-twentieth century. A mackintosh and leggings.

What gender is summer? Unlike spring, summer in its earliest uses was usually male – presumably a reflection of its grammatical status in Old English, where the noun *sumor* was masculine. The associations are always ones of vitality and jollity. Scots poet William Dunbar talks of 'lusty summer'. Edmund Spenser introduces 'jolly summer', and goes on to describe how 'on his head a

garland well beseen / He wore'. Shakespeare talks of 'summer and his pleasures' (in Sonnet 97). But during the seventeenth century we see increasing use of feminine pronouns, with associations of sensuousness and beauty: the season is often portrayed as a goddess or spirit representing the season's fertility. And for some poets, such as Emily Dickinson, summer is always female:

> Twice had Summer her fair Verdure
> Proffered to the Plain…

aestive

A word with two pronunciations: [ee] in the UK; [e, as in *met*] in the USA. And two spellings, for *e* is seen as an alternative early on, and became the preferred form in American English (as with other *ae/e* words, such as *encyclop(a)edia* amd *p(a)ediatrics*). It's from Latin *aestivus*, which had a range of uses all relating to summertime. Anything occurring in summer, or growing in summer, or intended for summer use, would attract the adjective. Many writers used it as a more impressive word for 'hot' or 'burning'.

It's recorded in English from the early seventeenth century, though another form, *aestival*, has citations dating from the fourteenth. It never seems to have been widely used. Nor were the associated forms that were coined during the same period. We see the noun *(a)estivation* for 'spending summer in a place', and sometimes used in a more specific way: a particular summer residence, or a place for summer pasturing. There's a verb *(a)estivate* 'to spend the summer'. In the nineteenth century these words developed specialized senses in botany and zoology – for example, an *(a)estivator* is an animal (such as worms and snails) that enters into a state of *(a)estivation*, adapting to hot or dry conditions. And in medicine a type of malaria that occurs in some regions in late summer and early autumn is described as *aestivo-autumnal* (see also p. 219).

Perhaps it is its rarity, along with its classical spelling, that has given *aestive* a certain social cachet. I've found it naming a London luxury travel agency and an Australian design studio. And in graphic design it names a sans serif font. But it's still rare – so much so that neither *aestive* or *estive* is allowed in playing Scrabble.

Barnabas Day

A traditional rhyme summarizes:

> Barnaby bright,
> The longest day
> And shortest night.

It's the feast day of St Barnabas, in the Christian tradition: the 11th of June. In the Old Style calendar this was the longest day. It was contrasted in another old rhyme with the shortest day, the 13th of December, the feast day of the fourth-century martyr St Lucy; 'Barnaby bright and Lucy light' (see p. 182).

Poets loved the alliteration and rhythm. Here's Edmund Spenser, in his ode *Epithalamion* (1595):

> Ring ye the bells, ye young men of the town,
> And leave your wonted labours for this day:
> This day is holy; do ye write it down,
> That ye for ever it remember may.
> This day the sun is in his chiefest height,
> With Barnaby the bright.

Barnabas, a Jew born in Cyprus, was one of Christ's earliest followers and is prominent in the biblical book known as the Acts of the Apostles as an energetic missionary, a close associate of St Paul. He was later a frequent choice as a name for a church or school, but he never became popular as a first name, apart from among parents who wanted a biblical name with positive associations. And among some musicians: it named an American Christian hard rock band of the 1980s. Several charities and missionary organizations have picked it up, such as *Barnabas Aid* and *Barnabas International*.

Its other shortened form, *Barney* – very different in tone – is much more common, and became famous in children's animated films and comics in such characters as Barney Bear and Barney the Dinosaur. Barnaby is also a popular choice, as its poetic use suggests. I've found it naming a ceramic collection and a shop selling homemade chocolate bars in London's Covent Garden. And in the Middle Ages there were *Barnaby fairs* – usually three-day events including the days before and after the eleventh. The market town of Macclesfield in Cheshire is one place that continues the tradition, though no longer in June, with its *Barnaby Festival*.

dog days

The expression arrived in English in the sixteenth century, a literal translation of Latin *caniculares dies*, 'canicular days', from *canis* 'dog', a root seen in the adjective *canine*, nicely glossed as 'doggish' in Henry Cockeram's *English Dictionary* of 1621 (which, incidentally, is the first time we see *dictionary* used in an English book title).

Why dog? In Greek and Roman mythological astronomy, Sirius, the brightest star in the constellation Canis Major ('greater dog'), was known as the 'dog star' – obediently following his master Orion ('the hunter') into the night sky. Homer refers to it in Book 22 of the *Iliad*, when he describes Achilles racing over the plain with his bronze breastplate gleaming like Sirius: 'Orion's Dog, people call it, the brightest of all'. In the northern hemisphere Sirius rises in late July, though dates vary according to latitude. In the calendar included in the 1552 *Book of Common Prayer* the dog days are said to run between 7 July and 5 September.

It thus came to be associated with the hottest days of the year, and interpreted as an ominous time of ill health and other harmful effects – in popular tradition there was a widely held belief that this was a time when dogs would run mad, and thus present a risk of rabies. It was worse if it rained, as a folklore rhyme said:

> Dog days bright and clear
> Indicate a good year;
> But when accompanied by rain,
> We hope for better times in vain.

Eventually the expression ameliorated, and came to be used for any period of decline, reduced activity or difficult times. It's still used in this way, and sometimes in unexpected places. 'Dog Days Are Over' was a song by the British indie rock band Florence and the Machine in 2009.

Then, as happens so often with idioms, the phrase begins to be used literally, referring to activities for dogs at various times. *Dog Days Adventure* is a day-care centre (for dogs) in Surrey. All the seasons are there in the titles of books, journals and podcasts: *The Dog Days of Spring*, *Autumn* and *Winter*, as well as *Summer*. There's a television film titled *The Dog Days of Christmas* (2021). That would have made no sense at all to our sixteenth-century forebears.

heatwave

I was expecting *heatwave* to be quite old, but in fact it isn't recorded in English until the 1840s, a time when the original meaning of *wave* (in relation to water movement) was noticeably broadening its figurative usage. Any sharp increase in the extent of something, over a relatively short period of time, attracted the word. We see it in *crime wave*, *waves of feeling*, and other such expressions, all appearing in the mid-nineteenth century. It's most often spelled as *heatwave* now, but *heat wave* and *heat-wave* are also used.

At first the word identified a period of abnormally hot weather that moved from place to place, whatever the season. There could be heatwaves in winter. But for most people today the term is associated with summertime – hence its presence in this section. The length of the wave is a variable, lasting for several days, or even a few weeks, according to region. If it's really short, it attracts the

prefix that became very popular during the second half of the twentieth century: a *mini-heatwave*.

Such a meaning is very easy to adapt, so it's hardly surprising that *heatwave* has come to name products associated with heat, such as sunglasses, radiators, milk warmers and thermal clothing. Also a brand of tortilla chips. It appeals to companies in the construction industry, especially if they're involved with heating installations. And it's named several films in cinema and television, with such themes as climate disaster and passionate romance.

It's also appealed to rock music fans, presumably because of the link between *heat* and *hot* in its modern senses of 'exciting', 'intense', 'energetic' (as in *hot jazz*). It named a London-based funk/disco group in the mid-1970s and a rock music festival held in Ontario in 1980. Music is also a major focus in a student-run radio station broadcasting from a Singapore Polytechnic. Its website strapline sums up the word's popular appeal: 'We are the hottest thing on campus.' Its name? *Radio Heatwave*.

high summer

High is a common Germanic word, and, in its earliest sense of 'extending far upward', it's there in Old English describing hills and mountains. But it was also used early on to describe the sun being 'high in the sky', and thus *high summer* meant the middle of summer, or its hottest period. *High noon* illustrates a similar development. (*Deep winter* shows the height scale being used in the opposite direction.)

It's proved to be a popular inspiration in art and music. Several paintings and prints have used the expression as a title. Norwegian painter Edvard Munch even used it twice: *High Summer 1* in 1902 and *High Summer 2* in 1915. In music, there are recordings with this name by a number of singers/songwriters, such as Van Morrison in 1999 and Joel Plaskett in 2024. The associations aren't always sunny. Morrison's lyrics are quite dark, as when a character in the song-story reflects on the way 'high summer' is 'lonesome' and 'gets him down'.

The number of artists who have used the name is far exceeded by the number of products that have adopted it – ranges of tableware and fabrics, lightweight gloves and bed linen, and various fashion designs and accessories. It named a 2024 clothing collection by English designer

Victoria Beckham, described by one fashion magazine with fulsome summery metaphors as 'a sun-drenched colour scheme of rustic browns, faded creams, and rusty terracotta reds, with gold accents lending an air of refinement'. It's an obvious description for seed growers, describing plants that are most productive during the peak summer months. And, perhaps even more obviously, for a shade of paint – yellow, of course.

Lammas

The harvest season in England traditionally began on the 1st of August – the 12th in the Old Style calendar – and was celebrated with a church service called in Old English *hlafmæsse*, from *hlaf* 'loaf' + *Mass*. It was a kind of harvest festival. On *Lammas Day* farmers made loaves of bread from the first wheat crop, and these were blessed in their local church. There might be feasts or festivities on *Lammas night*. The whole of August was *Lammas month*. But once *hlaf* ceased to be understood, some writers misconstrued it, thinking it had something to do with lambs, so we have such spellings as *Lambmesse*.

The name lives on for the time of year when the festival took place: *Lammastide* or *Lammastime*, the halfway point between the summer solstice and the autumn equinox (see pp. 11, 30). In Scotland, *Lammas* is one of the quarter days. The festival custom lasted until the Reformation, but there remains a celebration of bread and grain in modern Wiccan and pagan tradition. Some places still have *Lammas Fairs*, such as Exeter in Devon and St Andrews in Scotland. The *Ould Lammas Fair* in Ballycastle, Antrim, is rightly named, for it's the oldest fair in Northern Ireland. It achieved special fame when it became the subject of a ballad written by a local man, John Henry MacAuley, in the 1920s. This is its chorus:

> At the ould Lammas Fair, boys were you ever there?
> Were you ever at the Fair in Ballycastle-O?
> Did you treat your Mary Ann

to some Dulse and Yellow Man?
At the ould Lammas Fair in Ballycastle-O

That sweet-and-salty snack is a combination of local seaweed and a toffee-flavoured honeycomb, and is indeed bright yellow.

Lammas has had several specialized uses. In botany, *Lammas growth* – also known as *Lammas flush* or *Lammas leaves* – is a second growth of leaves in some species of trees in temperate climates during midsummer. In rural law, there are *Lammas lands* – so called because they were private property until Lammas Day, after which they became common land that could be used as pasture until the spring. Some are conservation areas now. And the environmental emphasis is also seen in a modern ecovillage in Pembrokeshire. They called it *Lammas*.

The name has been prominent in folklore. In some parts of Scotland and Ireland, from medieval times, couples married on Lammas Day would enter into a year-long union and then decide whether to make it permanent. And farmers eating a *Lammas bannock* (a type of cake) would throw a bit over their shoulder, asking a predator (such as a fox) to eat that rather than their livestock.

Lammas has two other claims to fame. According to Juliet's Nurse (in Shakespeare's *Romeo and Juliet*), the girl would soon be 14 years old, as she was born 'Of all days in the year come Lammas Eve at night'. And the Royal Mail in 1981 issued a 22p commemorative folklore stamp, with the name *Lammastide* proudly prominent. No other entry in this book has achieved such philatelic fame.

long hot summer

This common expression would have attracted no interest at all – except from the passing linguist – until it came to be associated with political issues. (Linguists would be intrigued by the adjective order, as the sequence sometimes turns up as *hot long summer*, and that sort of thing keeps them awake at night wondering why it doesn't feel right.)

The expression first came to public attention when it was used as the title of the 1958 film about racial tensions in the American South. The story was based on a novel by William Faulkner, published in 1940, *The Hamlet*. Book 3 of the novel is called 'The Long Summer'. They didn't use the novel's title, according to the director, Martin Ritt, to avoid any confusion with the Shakespeare play. The strapline in the film's release poster read: 'The people of Faulkner, the language of Faulkner, the world of Faulkner'. But *hot* was added, perhaps because of the influence of the hugely successful Pulitzer prize-winning play *Cat on a Hot Tin Roof*, by Tennessee Williams, which had recently (1955) been staged.

The expression took on a new lease of life a few years later, when the media began to use it to describe various summers in the 1960s when race riots took place in the USA. It then travelled to any place where there was public protest or industrial action during the summer months, when good weather attracted crowds. At one extreme it would describe rioting; at the other, behind-the-scenes dissent. Innumerable headlines used it, such as this one from the *Belfast Telegraph* in March 2017: 'PM finally triggers Brexit and we face a long, hot summer of discontent.'

The original film wasn't forgotten. It motivated a television series with the same title in the mid-1960s, and there was a remake in 1985. A different location, Ireland, is the theme of a 2015 novel by Kathleen MacMahon. But the vibe surrounding the expression hasn't always been gloomy. A British pop group of the 1980s, The Style Council, got the name into the hit music charts, as did another group, Girls Aloud, in 2005. And a London-based alternative rock band teamed up with Signature Brew, a company that specializes in music-inspired beers, to come up with a new lager during lockdown in the UK. As a brewery spokesperson commented: 'It's been a strange summer of cancelled gigs and festivals, so everyone needs a pint right now, and Long Hot Summer might just be the perfect beer for the season.'

(And in case you were wondering: grammatical principles do govern the sequence of adjectives in English. One is that those with the closest semantic relationship to the noun tend to stay near it – so *hot* is likely to be next to *summer*. Another is that adjectives of size usually precede others – we say *small round table* rather than *round small table*; *long curly hair*, not *curly long hair*. Taken together, *long hot summer* has to be the front runner.)

midsummer

The middle of summer – whenever that is. Today, in the northern hemisphere, it's usually felt to be in mid-July, and in the southern, mid-February. Its semantic range varies from a single day – traditionally the day of the summer solstice (p. 30) – to a period of indeterminate length, as seen in its derived forms.

The range of meaning is already apparent in the fourteenth century. We see its broadest application in the coinages *midsummer-time* and *midsummer-tide*, more restricted in *midsummer month*, and most of all in *Midsummer Day*, so named in Old English, albeit with a different period in mind (see p. 7), as was the evening of that day, *Midsummer Even* (later, *Eve*). *Midsummer Night* isn't recorded before the fourteenth century, but it soon became better known than its predecessors, thanks to Shakespeare's play *A Midsummer Night's Dream*.

The supposedly bad influence of midsummer heat led to an early association with strange behaviour and madness. In another of Shakespeare's plays, *Twelfth Night*, Olivia is horrified by the unusual behaviour of Malvolio: 'this is very midsummer madness', she exclaims. In the early sixteenth century the poet laureate John Skelton called it *midsummer maze* in his long autobiographical dream poem *The Garden of Laurel* – meaning a state of amazement. The full moon at midsummer was often felt to be responsible. In Act 4 of John Dryden's comedy *Amphitryon* (1690), Mercury refuses to recognize his master, who harangues him:

'What's this Midsummer-Moon? Is all the World gone a-madding?'

The word has been the source of a few other coinages. *Midsummerish* had some use in the nineteenth century, and is still heard, but it's lost out to *midsummery*. *Midsummer* is occasionally used in botany, such as for the ox-eye daisy, which is sometimes called *midsummer daisy*. Unusually, for seasonal words, the old spelling of the word, *midsomer*, has had a modern renaissance. I've found it naming a quilting company, a variety of mead, a kitchen range, and a company dealing with solar panels, and it's quite popular as a name for holiday accommodation. But nothing matches the reach of this spelling since it was chosen for the hugely successful ITV crime drama television series, *Midsomer Murders*, aired since 1997, and set in the fictional English county of Midsomer. Several of the villages there have it as part of their names, such as Midsomer Wellow. The spelling neatly reflects rural English reality and Old English etymology (*sumor* 'summer'): there's a real one in Somerset, *Midsomer Norton*.

St Swithun's Day

He was an Anglo-Saxon Bishop of Winchester in the ninth century, and one of the earliest English saints. His name is found with alternative spellings, *Swithun* and *Swithin*. I use the former, reflecting its widespread use in Winchester and nearby areas, where it names churches, schools, streets and, most famously, St Swithun's Bridge in the city, supposedly built at his suggestion. The name is from Old English *swiþ* [pronounced sweeth], meaning 'strong' or 'powerful'.

He earns an entry in this book because of the way his feast day, the 15th of July, has entered English folklore, and thus the language as a whole. Many old rhymes summarize the legend, this one from Scotland being one of the most quoted:

St Swithun's day, if thou dost rain,
For forty days it will remain;
St Swithun's day, if thou be fair,
For forty days 'twill rain nae mair.

Some accounts require a more specific location for the legend to be efficacious: it has to rain on his bridge.

The history of the legend is obscure, but there's a weather hint in the writing of the twelfth-century English historian (writing in Latin) William of Malmesbury. In Book 2 of his *Gesta Pontirficum Anglorum* ('Deeds of the English Bishops') he notes that Swithun asked for his body to be buried outside the Old Minster in Winchester, 'where it would be subject to the feet of people passing by, and to the raindrops pouring from above'.

Whatever the belief, meteorological science fails to support it. Some writers have been fierce in their scepticism, such as the eighteenth-century poet and playwright John Gay, who condemned it in his long poem *Trivia: or The Art of Walking the Streets of London*

(1716). In his Book 1 he includes 'signs of the weather', and attacks the 'superstition' that associates the feasts of Saints Paul and Swithun with weather conditions: 'Let not such vulgar Tales debase thy Mind; / Nor Paul nor Swithin rule the Clouds and Wind' (*wind* rhymed with *mind*, in those days). I love the more judicious opinion on the website of the Royal Meteorological Society, MetMatters:

St Swithin's day if thou dost rain
For forty days, relatively unsettled
  there's a fair chance it will remain
St Swithin's day if thou be fair
For forty days, a northerly jet stream
  might result in some fairly decent spells
But then again it might not.

strawberries and cream

Berry and *cream* are straightforward: the first is a common Germanic word, found in Old English; the second is a borrowing from Old French in the fourteenth century. *Straw* is more of a problem. It's also Germanic, and is there in Old English (*streaw*), but no other Germanic language uses it to describe the fruit (they go in for a compound to do with 'earth', as in German *Erdbeere* and Danish *jordbær*). Why *straw*? Was it the scattered appearance of the external seeds that reminded people of straw strands? Or the leaf clusters and stalks? Or an association between the fruit and layers of straw used as a form of protection during their growth? You choose.

Asked to choose about this expression's association with summertime, and there's no uncertainty. In 2024 British sweet-maker Swizzels carried out a survey. Which are the top flavours and foods associated with a British summer? *Strawberries and cream* came out far ahead of anything else, with 62 per cent. And then they asked the question addressing the connection that most people immediately associate with it: Which sports are most associated with a British summer? The answer might be a surprise: tennis, with 65 per cent, well ahead of cricket. And, if asked, the answer could have been more specific: Wimbledon, where the delicacy was offered from the beginning of the tournament in 1877.

The history of the dish is full of stories. The front runner is certainly Cardinal Thomas Wolsey, who is said to have introduced it to the court of Henry VIII in the early sixteenth century, and thus given it a fashionable cachet. Tudor doctor Andrew Boorde included it in his *Dyetary of Helth* (1542), the first printed book on healthy dieting: 'Raw cream, undecocted, eaten with strawberries ... is a rural man's blanket' – he means a comfort food. And he adds: 'I have known such blankets hath put men in jeopardy of their lives' – though it's a matter of conjecture whether this remark is a satirical jibe at its popularity or a serious warning against overeating.

By the end of the sixteenth century it was being routinely celebrated. At the beginning of George Peele's play *The Old Wives' Tale* (1595), a fairy song is heard:

> Whenas the rye reach to the chin,
> And chopcherry, chopcherry, ripe within,
> Strawberries swimming in the cream,
> And schoolboys playing in the stream...

And the celebrations and innovations continue. In 2025 Marks & Spencer announced a limited edition of a strawberries-and-cream sandwich, evidently inspired by the popularity of the dish in Japan. It's not recorded who in the United States instituted National Strawberries and Cream Day on 21 May, or when, but I don't care. It's a good excuse.

summer games

Today, this expression usually bring to mind sporting events held during the summer months, notably the Summer Olympic Games, often capitalized and shortened to *Summer Games* – an essential adjective after *Winter Games* were introduced in the 1920s. But the notion of 'summer games' in English, identifying a folk festival, goes back to the Middle Ages. They were usually held at midsummer, with dancing, minstrels, games, performances and general merrymaking. In some parts of the country, a *summer game light* would be lit in the parish church on Midsummer's Day (p. 104).

The games didn't always get a good press. The fourteenth-century chronicler Robert Mannyng was in no doubt. He writes in his long devotional poem *Handling Sin*:

> Dances, carols, summer games,
> Of many such come many shames.

In Chaucer's *Canterbury Tales*, the Wife of Bath includes a story of a Roman man who is so appalled that 'his wife was at a summer's game / Without his witting [*knowledge*]' that he leaves her! And in the diocese of York in 1569 an admonition was issued for local parishes to be 'circumspect what licences you give to persons to keep common summer games, for we hear of some great abuses therein'. Two years later there was a more explicit warning: 'the minister and churchwardens shall not suffer any lords of misrule or summer lords or ladies or any disguised persons … or any minstrels, morris dancers or others'. Presumably as a result of such constraints, along with later Puritan disapproval, references to the festivals died away during the seventeenth century.

But the notion of a festival lives on today in the video games industry. In 2020 Canadian game journalist Geoff Keighley introduced a series of global events to provide an outlet for news and demos. Begun at a difficult time (coronavirus) for public events, it has become an annual occasion held in early June. It's called *Summer Game Fest*.

summer house

It's been recorded in English since Anglo-Saxon times, with the obvious meaning of a residence used in summertime, though its character and function altered greatly over the centuries. We see it written both spaced and solid (*summerhouse*). In early use, the place could be near the house used during the rest of the year. Later it would be further away, in some pleasant location. In the sixteenth century it begins to be used for any small building designed for use in fine weather, such as in a public park or seaside promenade, or privately in a large garden. It's that last context which is the dominant one today. All kinds of garden summer houses are available online.

Linguistically, the expression was consolidated when it was used in the first Bible translations, such as those associated with Wyclif in the fourteenth century, Coverdale in the sixteenth and King James in the seventeenth. In the book of Amos (chapter 3) an angry God threatens to 'smite the winter house along with the summer house'. That was in the Middle East. Hotspur, in Shakespeare's *Henry IV Part 1*, provides an English example: he sounds off about Glendower's tedious oratory:

> I had rather live
> With cheese and garlic in a windmill, far,
> Than feed on cates [*delicacies*] and have him talk to me
> In any summer house in Christendom.

Evidently Glendower could ruin even the pleasantest getaway.

The positive associations of a summer house are widespread in the products that have used the name – several brands of fabrics and clothing, soft drinks, and ranges of relevant equipment, such as rugs, table linen and tableware. But beware! Things can happen in summer houses, ranging from the fearsome through the foreboding to the flirtatious. For the first: James Patterson's thriller murder mystery *The Summer House* (2020). For the second, Alice Thomas Ellis's trilogy (1991) of the same name – a story told from different points of view by three women narrators. And for the third, the American TV reality series (aired since 2017), where a group of New Yorkers, trying to escape the stresses of city life, find (as the IMDB website puts it) 'the only things guaranteed are sun, fun, and drama'.

summer pudding

The English word *pudding* has had a wide appeal; it's been borrowed by several European languages, often without change, such as *le pudding* in French or *der Pudding* in German. But where did the English get it from in the first place? Ironically, from French, in the thirteenth century, and – vegetarians/vegans look away now – in an intestinally meaty sense. It came from *bodin* (in various spellings), which was a kind of sausage – a sense still encountered in some regional dialects, and in standard English in *black pudding*.

It seems to have been the idea of something being encased that led to the modern meaning. Sausages are meaty preparations enclosed in a skin of some kind. The practice was then extended to other things. In the sixteenth century, fireworks were sometimes called *puddings*. And in the same century we see the word used for a mix of sweet or savoury ingredients steamed or baked in a bag or piece of cloth. It was a short step then to apply *pudding* to any sweet mixture. Prefixes soon followed, to identify types and regions, such as *bread pudding*, *plum pudding*, *Yorkshire pudding*, and these proliferated in the nineteenth century.

The twentieth century saw further linguistic developments. *Pudding* gained a new use as a mass noun ('What's for pudding?'). And there were serious social disputes over the fashionable way to refer to the 'pudding course' in a meal. *Dessert* had been borrowed from French in the seventeenth century (from *desservir* 'remove dishes from the table'), and *sweet* was a further alternative in the nineteenth ('What will you have for sweet?').

Summer pudding echoes the encasement theme of earlier times: mixed soft summer fruits usually enclosed in juice-soaked bread. It's first recorded in 1875, as part of the Victorian boom in prefixed puddings. Its mixed colours then made it an appealing name for any products where colour variation is intrinsic or designed, such as paints, wool, flower collections, scented candles, patterned paper and place mats. It's a natural name for a kind of jam, an intriguing name for a brand of gin and a delightful name for a cuddly bear. The last was a limited edition from Charlie Bears, an English company specializing in collectable bears, and – pun alert – part of a collection they called 'Everything is Pawsible'.

summer time

It has to be two words, separately stressed, to avoid a clash with *summertime*, and it's often capitalized. It can be prefixed, as in *British Summer Time*, and then it has its own abbreviation, BST. Its linguistic interest is chiefly historical, though not to any great extent.

The practice of adding one hour to Greenwich Mean Time (GMT) dates only from the early twentieth century. *Daylight saving time* is first recorded in 1908; *British summer time* in 1916. The expression was adapted just once, during World War II: the summer months between 1941 and 1945 added two hours – *Double Summer Time*. It operated again in 1947, motivated by the fuel shortages following an exceptionally hard winter. There was also an experiment in Britain in 1968 to keep GMT+1 throughout the year, but three years later it was cancelled. That hasn't stopped proposals being regularly raised in Parliament to drop it.

The arguments in favour go back further than the actual term. The American statesman, scientist and writer Benjamin Franklin is given the credit for first spelling them out, in an anonymous letter to the first French newspaper, the *Journal de Paris*, in 1784. He begins:

> I was the other evening in a grand company, where the new lamp of Messrs. Quinquet and Lange was introduced, and much admired for its splendour; but a general inquiry was made, whether the oil it consumed was not in proportion to the light it afforded, in which case there would be no saving in the use of it.

He puzzled over this that night, until…

> An accidental sudden noise waked me about six in the morning, when I was surprised to find my room filled with light; and I imagined at first, that a number of those lamps had been brought into it; but, rubbing my eyes, I perceived the light came in at the windows.

Realizing it was an early sunrise, he then estimates the cost 'that the city of Paris might save every year, by the economy of using sunshine instead of candles'. It was 96 million French pounds (*livres*). But it was well over a century before the world took his reasoning on board.

summer sayings

- One swallow does not make a summer.
- Summer is a seemly time.
- It is not summer until the crickets sing.
- Do what we can, summer will have its flies.
- The summer insect knows not ice.
- Look for summer on the top of an oak tree.
- As light as a summer cloud.
- For age and want save while you may,
  No summer's sun lasts a whole day.
- An English summer – two fine days and a thunderstorm.

O thou who passest thro' our valleys in
Thy strength, curb thy fierce steeds, allay the heat
That flames from their large nostrils! thou, O Summer,
Oft pitched'st here thy golden tent, and oft
Beneath our oaks hast slept, while we beheld
With joy thy ruddy limbs and flourishing hair.

Beneath our thickest shades we oft have heard
Thy voice, when noon upon his fervid car
Rode o'er the deep of heaven; beside our springs
Sit down, and in our mossy valleys, on
Some bank beside a river clear, throw thy
Silk draperies off, and rush into the stream:
Our valleys love the Summer in his pride.

Our bards are fam'd who strike the silver wire:
Our youth are bolder than the southern swains:
Our maidens fairer in the sprightly dance:
We lack not songs, nor instruments of joy,
Nor echoes sweet, nor waters clear as heaven,
Nor laurel wreaths against the sultry heat.

William Blake, 'To Summer', 1783

AUTUMN/ FALL

I love to wander through the woodlands hoary
In the soft light of an autumnal day,
When Summer gathers up her robes of glory,
And like a dream of beauty glides away.

How through each loved, familiar path she lingers,
Serenely smiling through the golden mist,
Tinting the wild grape with her dewy fingers
Till the cool emerald turns to amethyst;

Kindling the faint stars of the hazel, shining
To light the gloom of Autumn's mouldering halls,
With hoary plumes the clematis entwining
Where o'er the rock her withered garland falls.

Sarah Helen Power Whitman (1803–78),
'A Still Day in Autumn'

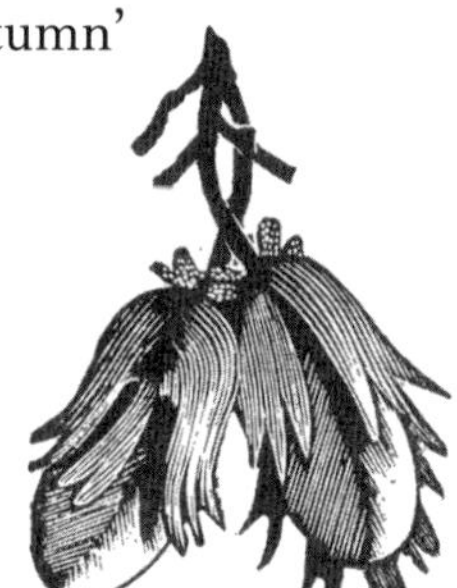

autumn/fall

Why does this season have two names? British people usually say *autumn* and Americans usually say *fall*. In some countries, people say both – Canada, for instance, reflecting British history and American adjacency, with *autumn* conveying a somewhat more formal tone. And in countries where *autumn* is traditional (such as India), *fall* is increasing its presence, especially among youngsters, due to American cultural influence.

Autumn is first recorded in texts from around 1400, with some writers borrowing it directly from Latin *autumnus* and some from French *automne*. But before that century was out, a new expression came into use to describe this period of the year: *falling of the leaf*. By the mid-1500s, *falling* in that phrase had shortened to *fall*. It was routine to use this in a listing of the seasons, as seen in educational writer Roger Ascham's 1545 dialogue about archery, *Toxophilus* (the name means 'lover of the bow'): 'The whole year is divided into four parts, springtime, summer, fall of the leaf, and winter.' Soon after, there was a second shortening, resulting in *fall* or *the fall*.

What's important to appreciate is that both *autumn* and *fall* were used in Britain in the sixteenth and seventeenth centuries. Nobody could have been more British than the sixteenth-century essayist William Cornwallis, born in Norfolk, who became a courtier and a Member of Parliament. In a 1601 essay 'Of traps for Fame', he introduces an analogy with fishermen, who have 'flies for the spring, the fall, and the winter'.

Both words crossed the Atlantic with the early settlers, and usage preferences went in different directions during the 1600s. By the end of the century, *autumn* had become the dominant form in British English; and by the end of the following century *fall* had become the norm in the USA – though *autumn* was still used. Today in Britain, *autumn* is the standard form; but *fall* will still be heard regionally. Joseph Wright recorded over thirty instances, from Scotland to Somerset, in his *English Dialect Dictionary* (1906), along with an interesting *fall-rains* in Devon. That was 1896. Do people still say it, I wonder?

Autumn has continued to generate new usages. In the fifteenth century we find *autumnal* and *autumnity*; in the sixteenth a short-lived *autumnian*. We begin to see it personified, usually relating to the bringing-in of a good harvest. All the recorded instances since are female. 'Autumn proudly bears her matron grace' writes Shelley in *Queen Mab* (1813). It's also used figuratively, suggesting middle age or the approach of old age, as in 'the autumn of one's years'. And then, as late as the nineteenth century, two more forms: *autumnize* for something having an autumnal appearance, and *autumny*, for anything resembling autumn.

Which leave just one question. What did people say before *autumn* and *fall* arrived, if they wanted to talk about the transitional period between summer and winter? See the entry on *harvest* (p. 130).

> Season of mists and mellow fruitfulness,
> Close bosom-friend of the maturing sun.
>
> John Keats, 'Ode to Autumn', 1819

All-Hallows see ***Halloween***

back end

I remember hearing this name for autumn when I lived in Lancashire in the 1950s. It was a shortening of 'back end of the year', which is how the word was used when it first came into English in the late sixteenth century, spaced, hyphenated, or solid (*backend*). But the expression could apply to the later stage of any period of time: for example, people would talk about 'the back end of the week', which might be any time from Thursday to Sunday. It seems to be an older generation's usage now.

It could also be used for any season, but in Scotland, and throughout the north and midlands of England, the focus was on autumn, late autumn and sometimes early winter. Its extent wasn't fixed: for some, *back end* finished at Martlemas (p. 184); for others, it went well beyond it, to the end of the year. There's an old saying in Yorkshire that the year consists of nine months of winter and three months of back end.

Occasionally, events would attract the name. Festivals in late autumn were sometimes called *back end fairs*. And *backendish* was a common description for a wet and windy day at that time of year. Some think the phrase shows the influence of Danish, given the long-term presence in the east of England's *Danelaw* in Anglo-Saxon times. Certainly modern Danish has a word *bagende* referring to the latter part of any period.

In the late seventeenth century the expression came to be applied to the rear part of an object or machine and contrasted with *front end*. The twentieth century saw several specialized senses emerge, most famously in the 1960s in relation to computing, for the hardware and software that work 'behind the scenes'. Say *back end* these days, and most people think digital rather than seasonal.

churn supper

This is one of several regional expressions to describe the evening feast after the last sheaf of a harvest is brought in. (*harvest-home* (p. 131) was the most widely used expression for such merrymaking, and the oldest recorded, from the sixteenth century.) *Churn* is a common Germanic word, and is found from Old English onwards in its basic sense of a vessel for making butter; but its function as a container for cream isn't recorded before the early 1800s. At a *churn supper*, the container would be circulated around the rustic assembly, and everyone would dip their bread or cake into it. In some places the evening was called a *churn-getting*.

Slightly earlier, in Scotland and parts of northern England, the expression was *kirn-supper* – a word that may be an old variant of *churn*, or perhaps related in some way to *corn*. I think the former is more likely. *Church* and *kirk* show a similar sound change. In the south-west of England the last sheaf was called a *neck* or *knack*. It would be welcomed with cheering: the reapers would *hollo* or *hail the neck*.

Another variant recorded in the eighteenth century was *mell-supper*, again from the north, and also found in the north of Ireland. *Mell* was another name for the last sheaf. Its etymology is unknown, though there are several spellings, such as *mall* and *meal*, which give a hint. There was cheering here too: *shouting the mell*. Joseph Wright, in his *English Dialect Dictionary* (1906), records a rhyme from the mid-nineteenth century:

Bless the day that Christ was born,
We've getting't mell of [*name of the farmer*]'s corn
Well bound and better shorn.
Huzzah! [*and variants*]

guy

Although the event that led to the use of this word, the Gunpowder Plot, took place in 1605, there's no recorded use of the perpetrator's first name, used alone, until 1796. The failed event had been celebrated annually with bonfires and fireworks, along with a scarecrow-like effigy of Guy Fawkes; but his name was always spelled out in full. In the mid-eighteenth century, people began to use it for the 5th November: *Guy Fawkes Day/Night*, soon shortened (as often today: 'We've bought some fireworks for Guy Fawkes'), but again, always in full.

Around 1800 we see the first name appearing on its own as a common noun. It was always disparaging. A badly dressed man could be called a *guy*, or anyone treated as a figure of fun. It was a sense that lasted into the twentieth century, but it then died out as other senses developed – the ones that dominate today.

The process started in the United States. Why there? Allan Metcalf puts it nicely in *The Life of Guy* (2019):

> Americans ... found it difficult to focus on Fawkes as the arch-traitor, considering that they too had aimed to overthrow the British government. It was also hard for Americans to get excited about a man across the ocean, two centuries earlier, who was trying to do more or less what Americans had been doing in the Revolutionary War.

During the nineteenth century we see *guy* steadily increasing its semantic range – first as a way of addressing a man; then in the plural, for a group of men; and then in the late twentieth century for any kind of group, male or female. Even animals could be so addressed ('Look at those little guys...'). The word lost its disparaging connotations, and gathered adjectives: *a good guy*, *some interesting guys...*

The American usage soon crossed the Atlantic, where in British English it spread alongside the traditional usage. As the 5th of November approached, children would go about with an effigy asking 'penny for the guy', to buy fireworks – though the custom seems to be dying out, due to age restrictions on firework purchase.

Why did *you guys* become so widespread so quickly? A linguistic answer would draw attention to the gap in the English pronoun system left by the loss of *thou* in all but a few religious settings. In its earliest use, *thou* was used for addressing one person, with *you* for more than one. Once *thou* was no longer in everyday use, there was a potential ambiguity. Who's being addressed if someone says 'Are you ready?' One or more? 'Are you guys ready?' solved the problem.

Halloween

Today, this is the universally known name for the evening of the last day of October. Its spirit is ancient, but this form of the word isn't. It's first recorded in the sixteenth century as *hallow even* or *eve*. *Even* was colloquially shortened to *e'en* at the time, but we don't see *Hallowe'en*, with or without the apostrophe, until the late eighteenth century. By then, the sense had narrowed to 'evening'. (In Shakespeare's day, *e'en* included afternoon as well. In his *Romeo and Juliet*, the Nurse bids Mercutio *good morrow* – 'good morning'. He replies with *good e'en*. The Nurse is surprised: 'Is it good e'en?' And in a bawdy reply he tells her that the clock is showing noon.)

The first part of the name is common to the Germanic languages, and in Old English is one of a cluster of words all expressing a notion of holiness. *Holy* had a long vowel in Old English – *halig* [pronounced hah-likh] – and this 'a'-quality remained in *hallow*, used both as a verb, 'to make holy', and as a noun, 'a holy person', and specifically a saint. The 1st of November was celebrated as the feast day of all the saints, *All Hallows* – found in its full form of *All Hallowmas* in the 1400s, and shortened in a different way as *Hallowmas*. That *-mas* ending (from the Catholic celebration of Mass) was common in those days to express the notion of a church festival or saint's feast day. We see it elsewhere in this book (*Candlemas*, *Lammas, Michaelmas*, *Christmas*, pp. 159, 100, 137, 162).

From the sixteenth century on we see references to *hallow-tide*, *hallow-fairs*, and *hallow-fires*, along with *hallow-eve* and *hallow-day,* the last recorded in dialects well into the twentieth century. But nothing matches the take-up of *halloween* as the name for the range of present-day activities in some countries of playing pranks, wearing costumes, lighting lanterns, and presenting all kinds of ghostly and ghoulish decorations and entertainments.

Many of these practices have been related to ancient pre-Christian customs. In the Old Celtic calendar, the last night of October was the final night of the old year, a time between summer and winter when it was believed the spirits of the dead could appear. It was called *Samhain* [pronounced sown] – a name of uncertain etymology, possibly meaning 'summer end', or perhaps relating to an Indo-European root meaning 'gathering' (that is, of the living and the dead). Festival-goers would wear masks or disguises (to hide themselves from witches or evil spirits), and light fires (to keep them away).

Halloween-tide has also expanded its time-range (another example of holiday creep: see p. 165). You can go on a *Halloween cruise*, beginning at the end of September. And some shops now begin selling *halloweenware* as early as July or August. It's given us the latest coinage: *Summerween*.

Hallowmas see ***Halloween***

harvest

As you would expect, with such a fundamental human activity, the word is found in all the Germanic languages, and it's there in Old English from the ninth century, identifying the season we now call *autumn* (see p. 121), thought of as the time of year for reaping and gathering in ripe grain. Once that sense had been left behind, replaced by *fall* and *autumn* in the Middle Ages, *harvest* developed

its own lexical family. We see *harvest-time* (and *-tide*) and *harvest month*, and the very popular *harvest home*, for the successful bringing in of the last of the harvest, and the merrymaking that celebrated it.

People names proliferated. By the sixteenth century we see *harvest wench*, *harvest woman*, *harvest swain* and *harvestman* (for the labourer, not the long-legged spider – that's a nineteenth-century name). The farm owner or the chief reaper would be called the *harvest-lord*, and his wife – or a woman given the honour – the *harvest-lady* or *harvest-queen*. An alternative phrasing as *lord of the harvest* became especially familiar, thanks to its use in the sixteenth-century translations of the Bible, beginning with William Tyndale in 1526 and consolidated by the King James Bible of 1611. In the Gospels of Matthew and Luke, God is described as *the Lord of the harvest* – that is, needing labourers to work on his behalf.

This was one of the earliest metaphorical uses of the noun *harvest*. It even became proverbial: 'to make a long harvest of a little corn' is listed in a seventeenth-century collection by the English naturalist John Ray. But it's the verb use, *to harvest*, that proved to be especially productive, especially in the twentieth century. The notion of harvesting crops is a distant memory, as virtually anything can be harvested nowadays. We can harvest useful substances, such as rainwater; cells and body organs for medical purposes; animal numbers to reduce populations; and even abstract notions, such as strategies in the investment world. The latest use is the most prolific: the automatic electronic harvesting of data by organizations, especially in the context of AI.

The positive connotations of *harvest* have given it a wide appeal. There are hundreds of *Harvest* names out there, often with well-being in mind, such as companies dealing with renewable energy, healthcare equipment, wealth management or religious groups. Digital well-being is prominent too: the word names several hardware and software solutions. And it's gone off into space, with NASA Harvest – a consortium, brought together in 2017, providing data from satellite Earth observation to gain insights into agriculture and food supply.

hay

This is another Germanic word for an ancient agricultural practice: cutting grass and drying it for later use as fodder. It appears in some of the earliest Old English texts, along with its store place, *hay-house*. There's then a puzzling gap in the records until the early 1500s, when a whole family of derived words appear. One of the first was *haymaker* (the person, not the swinging blow in boxing, which was American slang in the late nineteenth century). The time of year when hay is cut is seen in *hay-time* and later *hay-season*, along with *haymaking* and *hay-harvest*. The result of the process is seen in *haystacks*, *haycocks* and *hayrigs* – all in use during the sixteenth century. That period also sees a verb, *to hay*.

Its fundamental role in agricultural life is reflected in its emerging proverbial status. One of the earliest, listed in a collection of proverbs in 1546, is *make hay while the sun shines* – 'lose no time', 'seize the moment'. Another is *look for a needle in a haystack* (earlier, *in a bundle of hay*). The idiomatic growth continued into the nineteenth century, with *make hay*, meaning 'throw into confusion'. Then in the twentieth we see the most widely used expressions: *hit the hay* for 'go to bed'; *a roll in the hay* for 'love-making'; the American negative colloquialism for a lot of money, *that ain't hay*; and the very common *go haywire*.

Haywire started in the USA, literally meaning the wire used to bind bales of hay together. But then people started to use that kind of wire to carry out any kind of makeshift repair, so it gradually took on the meaning of 'anything inefficient'. To *go haywire* thus meant 'go seriously wrong' or 'be out of order'. And the final stage, by the 1930s, was when this was applied to people in an emotional state, especially if they were acting in an incompetent or crazy way.

But it's been reclaimed, with people moving it away from negative situations, adapting the unconventional element in the earlier sense to make it work in forward-looking contexts. It's named various music bands and albums, innovative restaurants and appealing comic-book characters. And people have begun to play with the spelling. An American electronic music performer has given himself the stage name of *Haywyre*. And in 1998 the Australian Broadcasting Corporation (ABC) introduced an initiative – as its website puts it – 'to give young regional, rural and remote students the opportunity to enter the national discussion, where they are often unheard and under-represented'. In a brilliant piece of linguistic creativity, they called it *Heywire*.

Indian summer

The expression is North American in origin, recorded from the late eighteenth century; but there's no consensus as to why this name was chosen to describe a period of unusually warm and dry weather in late autumn (in the northern United States). It may simply have been an association of ideas – that such weather was noticed in regions occupied by Native American communities, or with a late hunting season. But the phenomenon was so distinctive that the expression soon travelled widely – into England by the mid-nineteenth century, though it didn't achieve widespread use until a century later.

It then developed a second life, used figuratively to describe a time in the later life of a person characterized by peacefulness and calm, or a newfound romantic relationship. The latter is the heart of one of the stories in John Galsworthy's 'Forsyte Saga', *The Indian Summer of a Forsyte* (1918), exploring the friendship between young Irene and Old Jolyon. It's been applied historically to countries and organizations too, referring to a late flowering or renaissance of artistic, cultural, political or other achievements.

There have been a few other linguistic developments. The original expression was soon followed by *Indian-summerish*, and it's been used adjectivally, as in an *Indian summer afternoon*. In recent times in the USA, there's been a trend to avoid the name, as part of a climate of political correctness. It's no longer accepted by the American Meteorological Association, for instance, which recommends that *second summer* be used instead. In the nineteenth century, people described the opposite effect as *squaw winter*: a short early period of wintry weather, often preceding an Indian summer. That expression has also lost favour.

Indian summer has nonetheless been widely used in popular culture, with a long history of creative applications, especially by poets and musicians. There are over fifty songs or arrangements with this title, across the musical spectrum, such as by jazz pianist Dave Brubeck and Welsh rock band Manic Street Preachers, both in 2007. It was a favourite theme of Emily Dickinson, who succinctly captured the mood of gentle nostalgia in several poems, as in this opening stanza of 'Indian Summer':

These are the days when Birds come back—
A very few—a Bird or two—
To take a backward look.

In Britain, of course, there's a raft of associations not found in America, namely the historical links to the country of India. Several Indian restaurants have piggy-backed on the weather expression and named themselves with it. Also in Britain, there was a time when the expression was in competition with *St Luke's summer*, especially in southern regional dialects. It was sometimes qualified: *St Luke's little summer*. The meaning was the same, but the focus was on St Luke's feast day, the 18th of October. And there was another saint, associated with a later warming in November, but that's a winter's tale (see *Martinmas*, p. 183).

kirn-supper, mell-supper see ***churn-supper***

Michaelmas

The pronunciation has a short vowel (as in *Mick*), not the usual long vowel of the first name. We see it reflected in some of the medieval spellings, such as *Mickellmas*. It's a shortening of *Michael's Mass*, the first element referring to the archangel St Michael; the second to the principal Catholic celebration, and the whole to his feast day, usually 29 September. In the northern hemisphere it's close to the equinox (p. 11), and thus associated with the beginning of autumn.

The name, along with *Michaelmas Day* and *Eve*, is there in Anglo-Saxon times. *Michaelmas-tide* is recorded later, in the sixteenth century, though it would probably have been in much earlier use. *Michaelmas* soon came to be used in descriptions of autumnal nature. The harvest full moon was a *Michaelmas moon* (see also Appendix, p. 227). It named a species of autumn-flowering plant, the *Michaelmas daisy*, and a late-cropped vegetable, the *Michaelmas onion*. And in the eighteenth century it introduced yet another name for a period of unusually warm weather around this time (see also *Indian summer* above).

The feast day marked one of the quarter days in the legal calendar. From the fifteenth century it anticipated the start of a session of the High Court of Justice in England, as well as a new teaching period (*Michaelmas term*) in several schools and universities. As the first day in the farming year, tenant farmers would often give their landlord a *Michaelmas goose*, expressing their hopes for a prosperous year ahead.

The name also turns up in religious folklore. St Michael is the one who defeated the angel Lucifer, who fell from heaven and landed, so it is said, in a thorny blackberry bush. He spat on it and cursed its fruit, which explains why wild blackberries begin to grow mouldy around that time. As the Irish proverb puts it: 'On Michaelmas Day the devil puts his foot on blackberries.'

neck-supper see ***churn-supper***

reap

The action of cutting and gathering grain is so basic to agricultural practice that it's not a surprise to see the Anglo-Saxons using *reap-time* to mean 'harvest-time'; and *reaping-time* appears in early Middle English with the same sense. A cluster of person names followed: *reaper* and *reapman* in Old English; *reapster* in the fifteenth century. There was some variation in the forms of the verb. What is its past tense? Today, *reaped*. But there were regional variations, some of which can still be heard in dialects today, notably *reapen* and *rept* (for the latter, compare *leap* and *leaped/leapt*).

Its history as a figurative expression also began early. Shakespeare loved it, using *reap* not only with *harvest* but with abstract notions such as *fame*, *delights* and *thanks*. There's a literal application in *Henry IV Part 1*, when Hotspur describes a pompous lord: 'his chin new reaped / Showed like a stubble-land at harvest-home.' From the fourteenth century the verb developed a general sense of 'obtain an advantage', as in the present-day idiom *reap the benefit*. Shakespeare again: in *Twelfth Night* Olivia compliments the disguised Viola on his (*sic*) looks: 'When wit and youth is come to harvest / Your wife is like to reap a proper man.'

The growth in its figurative popularity was greatly stimulated by translations of the Bible, where we find it (in the influential *King James* version) over fifty times. It's there both as a reward for good works (as in the book of Psalms: 'They that sow in tears shall reap in joy') and as a punishment (as in the book of Jeremiah: 'They have sown wheat, but shall reap thorns'). The recurrent theme is one of justice, which motivated the proverbial saying that one reaps what one has sown – facing the consequences of one's actions.

The potentially negative side of reaping has appealed to modern authors. *The Reaping* has named a novel by Bernard Taylor (1980) and a horror film (2007). And it's there in the hugely successful *Hunger Games* series of dystopian novels by Suzanne Collins (2008 and after), with follow-up films. The latest, a prequel to the series, was published in 2025, and by the time you read this it will have come to a cinema near you: *Sunrise on the Reaping*.

Samhain see ***Halloween***
Saint Luke's summer see ***Indian summer***
squaw winter see ***Indian summer***

Thanksgiving

With a capital *T*, the word has only one meaning for most people: the day in the United States appointed for public acknowledgement of goodness received – divine goodness, in its original form, reflecting the religious faith of the Pilgrims; or goodness from any source, for those without a religious turn of mind. Celebrated on the fourth Thursday in November, it just earns its place in this section of the book – its equivalent in Canada even more so, for there it's held on the second Monday in October. And it has a similarly timed presence in some other countries too, especially those with historical links to the United States, such as Liberia and the Philippines.

Historically, the autumnal link is even clearer, for although the national holiday wasn't formally recognized until established by Abraham Lincoln in 1863, there has been a long-standing tradition that stems from the harvest festivals celebrated by the first settlers in the early seventeenth century, and in 1789 George Washington signed a proclamation for a 'day of public thanksgiving' in November. The general notion, of course, has an ancient presence, with every culture at some point making sacrifices or prayers to deities.

The Christian tradition is no different. It's recorded in England in the early sixteenth century in biblical translations and commentaries – William Tyndale is the first recorded user in 1533 – and the word consolidated its status in the *Book of Common Prayer.* It has only a passing presence in the 1552 version, for 'The thanksgiving of women after child-birth'; but in the 1662 edition it becomes a major section: 'Prayers & Thanksgivings upon several occasions'.

In the American setting, the word has entered into several combinations, reflecting the nature of the festivities, such as *Thanksgiving dinner* and *Thanksgiving turkey*, which are first recorded in the nineteenth century, and *Thanksgiving parades* in the early twentieth. There was even a short-lived verb, to *thanksgive*, in the seventeenth, which eventually lost out to *give thanks*, though I wouldn't be surprised to find it still in jocular use.

autumn sayings

- No more leaves fall in autumn than were grown in spring.
- Every leaf is a flower in the garden of fall.
- Leaves are falling, autumn is calling.
- Autumn is nature's way of saying 'Let's play'.

Autumn, that season of peculiar and inexhaustible influence on the mind of taste and tenderness
JANE AUSTEN, *Persuasion*, 1817

Autumn is a weathercock
Blown every way.
CHRISTINA ROSSETTI, 'Summer', 1866

Autumn wins you best by this, its mute
Appeal to sympathy for its decay.
ROBERT BROWNING, 'Paracelsus', 1835

As long as autumn lasts, I shall not have hands, canvas, and colours enough to paint the beautiful things I see.
VINCENT VAN GOGH, to his brother Theo, 1888

Fall, leaves, fall; die, flowers, away;
Lengthen night and shorten day;
Every leaf speaks bliss to me
Fluttering from the autumn tree.

I shall smile when wreaths of snow
Blossom where the rose should grow;
I shall sing when night's decay
Ushers in a drearier day.

Emily Brontë, 'Fall, Leaves, Fall', 1846

WINTER

O Winter! bar thine adamantine doors:
The north is thine; there hast thou built thy dark
Deep-founded habitation. Shake not thy roofs
Nor bend thy pillars with thine iron car.

He hears me not, but o'er the yawning deep
Rides heavy; his storms are unchain'd, sheathed
In ribbed steel; I dare not lift mine eyes;
For he hath rear'd his scepter o'er the world.

Lo! now the direful monster, whose skin clings
To his strong bones, strides o'er the groaning rocks:
He withers all in silence, and in his hand
Unclothes the earth, and freezes up frail life.

He takes his seat upon the cliffs, the mariner
Cries in vain. Poor little wretch! that deal'st
With storms; till heaven smiles, and the monster
Is driven yelling to his caves beneath Mount Hecla.*

William Blake, 'To Winter', 1783

* An active volcano in Iceland

winter

The word is in Old English, reflecting its origin in the Germanic family of languages. Various theories have been proposed about its etymology – links to other *w-* words such as *wind*, *weather*, *water*, *wet* – but no definite connection can be established. It's proved to be a hugely fruitful source of vocabulary, such as *winterly*, *midwinter* and *wintertide* in Old English; *winterlong* and *wintertime* in Middle English; *wintering*, *winterish*, *winter-like* and *winterous* in the sixteenth century; and so on, right down to the present day with *winterscape*, *overwinter*, *winter wonderland*, *nuclear winter*, and many more. I love the rarely used *unwinter*, first recorded in 1611: 'to get rid of winter'.

Then there are the conventional expressions, such as *winter coat*, *winter term* and *winter's tale* – the last best known for its Shakespearean presence – and dozens of plant names, such as *winter daffodil* and *winter jasmine*. But one of the most evocative expressions, to my mind, is in Old English: *wintercearig* [pronounced win-ter-chay-uh-rikh], literally 'winter-chary'. It's used in the poem *The Wanderer*, as the sad traveller describes his journey:

ic hean þonan I, dejected, from there
wod wintercearig travelled winter-weary
ofer waþema gebind over the ice-covered waves

ic hean þonan	I, dejected, from there
wod wintercearig	travelled winter-weary
ofer waþema gebind	over the ice-covered waves

Not all writers are so negative. The sixteenth-century Italian playwright Pietro Aretino wrote, in one of his letters (1537): 'Let us love winter, for it is the spring of genius' – meaning a time for introspection, imagination and healing. Evidently some authors get their best ideas in wintertime. Or perhaps it's simply that they find themselves with more time at home to write.

Unlike the other seasons, which vary in gender when personified in English, winter has always been portrayed as male since first being so recorded in the fifteenth century. It's usually an old man with grey or white hair, and he's often named: *Father Winter*, *Grandfather Winter*, *Old Man Winter*. The names have had a certain general appeal. I find *Old Man Winter* naming a racehorse, a bike rally, and at least three brands of beer. He sometimes has to compete for attention with another winter male: *Jack Frost* (p. 178).

There's a great deal of dialect and folklore ingenuity around the word *winter*. Several places have a custom called *bringing in winter*, where the person driving the last cart of harvest corn is given a special greeting – such as a bucket of water thrown over his face. Up in the north of Scotland there are *winter-steens* (stones). Here's a definition from the *Scottish Dialect Dictionary*:

a standing-stone or large boulder visited during the first winter moon by an unmarried person wishing to divine his or her future spouse by walking round it several times with and against the sun and reciting the names of desirable candidates.

And then there's the slang, such as this music-hall pun from the early 1900s. The idiomatic expression *winter draws on* (= winter's approaching) led to *winter drawers on*. It confuses anyone not familiar with this British slang term for 'knickers'.

The English winter – ending in July
To recommence in August...

LORD BYRON, *Don Juan*, 1837

Advent

For many, this word has no capital letter and a very general meaning: a slightly more formal way of referring to the arrival of something considered to be important. It's been used in that way since the sixteenth century. But long before that, in Old English, we see the capitalized form, borrowed from Latin *adventus*, to describe the Christian church season immediately before Christmas – Christ's festival. In the Western Church it's the preceding four Sundays, and since the eighteenth century the period has motivated several related expressions, such as *Advent candles* and *Advent wreaths*.

For an unknown but increasing number, though, the word has only one context: an *Advent calendar*. The earliest usage is mid-nineteenth century, and some sources think the popularity was due to its adoption by Queen Victoria and Prince Albert. Originally handmade, printed versions appeared in the early 1900s, the varying dates of the four Sundays being replaced by a standardized 24 days, beginning on the 1st of December. They took the form of twenty-four tiny windows or pockets, one opened daily. Each contained a message – at first, a verse from the Bible or an acknowledgement of the saints' days falling within the period; later, seasonal pictures, tiny gifts, or pieces of chocolate or other confectionary.

Today, what's revealed behind the window can be absolutely anything, depending on the calendar shape and size (and some are huge) – miniature whiskys, jewellery, cheese, tea, garden seeds, perfumes, toys, doggie treats, characters from children's stories... And I say 'increasing' above because they're also digital now, and online companies offer a remarkable range of options – a daily email, video, WhatsApp, text, photo, Instagram live... all brief and catchy, and thus of great appeal to those with short online attention spans.

It's not all virtual. There have been innovations in the physical world. Several places throughout the world now present 'living advent calendars'. A window or door is opened each day to reveal a festive scene or themed display, or a live performance of music, theatre, puppetry or story-telling. It's not only individual houses: shops, restaurants and other businesses can participate. And, thanks to social media, they can be viewed anywhere.

apple cider

Until the eighteenth century, *cider* always had an association with intoxicating liquor – the 'strong drink' referred to in the Bible, with Hebrew, Greek and Latin antecedents – *sicera* in Latin. The phonetic change of the medial consonant to [d] presents etymologists with a puzzle, but by the time the word entered English, from French, in the fourteenth century, it had settled down as *cider*. Being the fermented juice of apples, it came to be traditionally served after the apple crop, towards the end of the year, often heated, and thus widely thought of as a wintertime festival drink.

Apple cider might seem a tautology, but the adjective does help to distinguish it from other cider-like drinks, such as *pear cider* (*perry*), which also has a medieval history in English. When it's first recorded, in the seventeenth century, it still had its alcoholic association. That was the century when a wide range of related coinages appeared, such as *cider-press*, *cider-master*, *cider-mill* and *ciderist* (someone who makes cider or is knowledgeable about it). But in the United States during the eighteenth century it went in a new direction, for a non-alcoholic beverage. Fresh terminology followed alongside *apple cider*: *sweet cider* and *soft cider*, which prompted *hard cider* for the alcoholic version. *Cider*, when used alone, is thus now trans-atlantically ambiguous.

There have been several other derived words, such as *ciderish* and *cidery* in the nineteenth century; but linguistically there's nothing to match the coinage seen in Henry Fielding's novel *Joseph Andrews* (1742). Two of his characters have a merry morning as they drink 'a pot of cyder-and at the fire'. That's cider mixed with something else, presumably also alcoholic. It's rare indeed to see a conjunction used as a sort of suffix. The nearest I can think of is 'yes-and' thinking in brainstorming and (in the theatre world) improvising, where one follows up a suggestion with an additional constructive point. *Cider-and* never entered standard English, but I imagine it had a long life in British regional dialects.

apricity

It's a word that never caught on, and indeed its single citation in the *OED*, in Henry Cockeram's dictionary of 1623, suggests it may have been a lexicographer's creation, derived from Latin. In fact he gives two related words. *Apricitie* he defines as 'the warmness of the Sun in winter'. It's preceded by *aprication*: 'a beaking in the Sun' – from *beek*, an old Scottish and northern English word meaning 'suffuse with pleasurable warmth'. (*Bake* is probably related.) And later in the century we find an isolated use of *apricate*, 'to bask in the sun'.

Despite its apparent lack of use, over the centuries, *apricity* has had a twenty-first-century renaissance. The phonetic association with *April* has probably helped (though the month name has a different etymology; see p. 221). Type *apricity* into a search engine and you'll get hundreds of hits, with several websites referring to the meaning of the word, and its connotations, as the reason for their choice. A restaurant in Mayfair, London, explains its name as 'symbolizing regeneration, rejuvenation, generosity, and light'. A type of yarn 'reflects the comforting glow of sunlight on chilly days' and brings 'that same sense of warmth and light to your hands and your creations'. Doubtless a similar set of associations motivated its choice by companies offering ranges of ceramics and dress designs. It's also appealed to people in the medical world – for example, naming a healthcare company and a fertility clinic.

It's popular in the arts world too, labelling paintings by various artists, a literary and arts magazine from the University of Texas, a Canadian K-pop dance team and an Australian circus performance troupe, among others, all of them exploiting the metaphor of joy and warmth breaking through a dull, unresponsive or challenging world. The American composer Roger Zare chose it as the title for a piece he wrote in 2020, as the isolation of Covid approached, and he had 'a renewed appreciation for the warmth in my life'. And indeed, the notion did seem to capture the opportunities for renewed communicative interaction during the pandemic.

boreal

The word remembers *Boreas*, the Greek god of the north wind, and thus of winter and its associated cold and stormy weather. He starts to be mentioned in English in the fourteenth century in translations of Greek and Latin texts. The adjective arrived soon after. Anything relating to the northern hemisphere could attract the name, such as *boreal winter*, *boreal pole* and *boreal zodiac* (the constellations and signs visible in the north), and especially in the subarctic regions with their longer winters and distinctive vegetation, as in *boreal forests*.

Many people immediately associate the word with its Latin source in the atmospheric phenomenon of *aurora borealis*, the 'northern lights'. Go on a sailing trip to see them and you're likely to encounter the name sooner or later. There's a travel agency called *Boreal Expedition*, and a yachting company based in France (*Boréal*). And as I write these words (in 2025), I read that it names the latest SUV to come from Renault. The company website making the announcement explains: it's a name that 'conjures up visions of wide-open spaces and the power of the elements'.

There have been linguistic developments too: *hyperborean*, describing the extreme north of a northern country or the Earth as a whole; *sub-boreal*, for further south. There's also *Euroboreal*, recorded just once in the seventeenth century, but now adopted in ecology and climate science in relation to northern Europe (contrasting with *Eurotemperate* and *Eurotropical*). *Borealism*, as an ideology of northern peoples, histories and cultures, has come to be a politically loaded term in some countries.

The cold association has appealed to companies looking for a name for their cold-related products, as in air-conditioning and refrigeration, or for ways of coping with challenging weather conditions, such as anoraks, footwear and other equipment for climbing, hiking, trekking and trail running – *Boreal Europe* is an example. Some are quite explicit about it. *Boreal salt & pepper mills* (according to the website) 'draw their inspiration from Scandinavian design and the calm hues of boreal forests'. And the colours thought to be typically boreal – greens, blues, browns, greys, along with hues of black and white – predominate in products such as fabrics and tiles.

But there must be something about the sound of the word itself that gives it a more general appeal. I can't otherwise explain why it was chosen to name a perfume, a watch (*Boreal Blue*), and a real-estate investment management company (*Boreal IM*). And, in the world of printing, a typeface.

Boxing Day

Ask anyone in Britain and some other English-speaking countries, and they will have no problem identifying this as the day after Christmas Day. It's a public holiday, either on the 26th itself or on the following Monday if the 26th falls on a weekend. Ask anyone in the USA and you'll get blank looks, or a vague awareness that it's 'something British', and certainly no reason not to go back to work. Even in Britain, though, it's a fairly recent name: there would have been blank looks there too until the middle of the eighteenth century.

The original notion was philanthropic: a day when tradespeople would receive a present of some kind (usually money) from their customers, employees and apprentices from their employers, service staff from the master or mistress of a large house, and people in need from alms boxes in churches. The gift was originally (in the sixteenth century) called simply a *box,* and there was already a word (since the fifteenth) for the action of putting something into a box: *boxing*. There was also a custom for those playing a gambling game to put a portion of their winnings into a box, which was then given to the butler to store until Christmas (the *butler's box*), and it was a natural extension to call this a *Christmas box*. The butler practice seems to have died out during the seventeenth century, but not the label: by the beginning of the eighteenth, *Christmas box* was being used for any present given on 26 December, and the day received its modern name.

The most noticeable development in the twentieth century was the adjectival use of the expression, especially in relation to shopping and sports. There are *Boxing Day sales… races… fixtures… recipes… television… swims.* But the noun phrase isn't forgotten in popular culture. It's the title of several songs and paintings. And in 2021 it received its movie accolade, naming a British romantic comedy.

brumal

The very first citation in English for this word, from the early sixteenth century, highlights two semantic features: 'the short days that clerks clepe [*scholars call*] brumal'. *Brumal* is from Latin *brumalis*, 'belonging to winter', which in turn relates to *bruma* 'day of the winter solstice' and *brevis* 'short' – that is, the shortest day. Clerks were learned people, both clerical and lay. The implication is clear: *brumal* is a scholarly word.

It retained this tone in later use, typically in scientific discussion, but with some other uses among scholars, who appreciated its technical tone (as opposed to everyday 'wintry'), and poets, who loved its sound. The two words are indeed very different, phonaesthetically: *wintry*, with its short [i] and voiceless plosive [t]; *brumal* with its long [u:] and voiced continuants [m] and [l]. Hilaire Belloc, for example, in *September*, looks out of a window towards the site of the Battle of Sedan in 1870 and imagines an array of ghostly soldiers: 'A brumal army, vague and ordered large'.

The word has since had a certain appeal as a product name, with earlier connotations of gloom and melancholy being replaced by associations of warmth, comfort and resilience, as when it names a blend of coffee and a men's fleece. The most unusual use I've encountered has been in a periodical, edited from a university in Barcelona. Its full name in English: *Brumal-research Journal on the Fantastic.* Its website explains: to explore the 'confrontation between the real and the impossible in a textual world imitating ours' in a wide range of artistic media.

Brumal-derived coinages are uncommon. *Brumation* is the front runner, used in zoological research, referring to a state of winter dormancy exhibited by certain thin reptiles, such as snakes and lizards. It was coined in 1965 by American zoologist Wilbur W. Mayhew, who felt that there needed to be a special term, as opposed to *hibernation* (p. 173), to describe what he considered to be a distinctive physiological difference between cold- and warm-blooded animals. There was an associated verb, as seen in the heading to one article: 'Do reptiles hibernate or brumate?' The notion received criticism from those who felt that *hibernation* was a sufficient descriptor. But it's still quite widely used, and it wasn't long before painters, poets and dancers saw its relevance to such human states of mind as apathy, lethargy and lack of motivation, and used the word to explore themes of cyclicity, re-emergence and renewal. Jack Whiteley and Mathilde Lin's 2024 short dance film *Brumation* illustrates this direction. I suspect we'll see a lot more of this word.

Candlemas

A feast day with candles: *-mas* from the Catholic celebration of Mass, and *candle* from Latin *candela* [kan-day-la] and ultimately from *candere* 'to shine'. It's in the earliest Old English glossaries. The day is 2nd February, forty days after Christmas. It's variously described as the feast of the Purification of the Virgin Mary – a Jewish ritual in which new mothers went to the Temple to offer sacrifices – and the Presentation of Christ in the Temple, following the account in the Gospel of St Luke. In Christian tradition it was celebrated with a procession and display of candles, symbolizing Christ as 'the Light of the world' – a self-description in the Gospels of John and Matthew.

The day soon entered English as a whole as part of folklore. It was felt to be a special day, near to the end of winter, when people would look at the weather and make predictions about the arrival of spring. Good weather wasn't a good sign, as a Scottish rhyme summarized:

If Candlemas Day is bright and clear,
There'll be twa winters in the year.

Or this one, from England:

If Candlemas Day be fair and bright,
Winter will have another flight;
If Candlemas Day be shower and rain,
Winter is gone and will not come again.

Weather predictions turn up again in North America (see *Groundhog Day*, p. 169).

As that rhyme illustrates, the name came to be used (since the thirteenth century) in combinations; others are *Candlemas Eve* or *Even*, *Candlemas Night* and *Candlemas season*. It was especially productive in Scotland, in a variety of spellings, where several local gift-giving customs and bonfires (*Candlemas bleezes*, from *blaze*) are recorded in the eighteenth century – and probably go back much earlier.

Some schools had Candlemas customs. Students might bar the school gates, stop the schoolteacher from entering, and demand a holiday. Another practice is reported in the *Statistical Account of Scotland* (volume 12, 1794). Scholars attending the grammar school in St Andrews paid, in addition to their school fees, a *Candlemas gratuity* to the teacher. They would compete for the *Candlemas crown*. The *Candlemas king* (*Candlemas queen* for girls) was the one who was able to pay most. He reigned for six weeks, 'during which period he is not only intitled to demand an after-noon's play for the scholars once a-week but he has also the royal privilege of remitting all punishments'. Student power indeed.

Christingle

There's just one other entry in this book where a word has come into English directly from German, and it's related to this one. The story begins with the combination *Christ* + *Kind* ('child') + a diminutive suffix *l* or *le* – so, 'little Christ child'. The folk belief was that the baby Christ brings presents to children on Christmas Eve.

The name is found in English from the mid-nineteenth century, with two phonetic changes. The awkward [t] + [k] sequence was simplified to [t]; and the unfamiliar [dl] ending was replaced by *-ingle*. That was a familiar sound at an English Christmastime, thanks to the carol *Jingle Bells* and the American name for Santa Claus, *Kris Kringle* (that's the other German-sourced name: see p. 180); and probably the connotation of excitement expressed by *tingle* played a part as well. There may even have been an influence from the Scottish word *ingle*, meaning a 'fire' – the kind that burns in a house fireplace – which has a history from the sixteenth century.

Whatever the origins, the contemporary use is really a mid-twentieth-century development, when it became a church service for children, adopted chiefly by the Church of England Children's Society and held during the Advent season. Candles were a central feature. The usual practice was to give each child a symbolic lighted candle (= Christ as the light of the world) set into an orange (= the planet Earth) and decorated with fruit and nuts (= the produce of the land). What's linguistically interesting is that the objects were also named *Christingles*. So one could hear sentences in which the name was used in two grammatical ways: 'Let's make some Christingles for Christingle'.

Christmas

The central role played by Christmas in religious and cultural settings is reflected in the remarkable number of derived words and idioms that have come into English, making it the longest entry in this book. Its original meaning is reflected in some of the earliest spelling in Old English, such as *Cristesmæsse* – 'Christ's Mass', the Catholic eucharistic celebration, viewed as an event of special significance on the day traditionally assigned to the birth of Jesus, 25 December. The possessive sense is also there in the form *Christenmas*, recorded in the fourteenth century in Scotland and northern England, and later in Ireland, and still in sporadic dialect use in the twentieth century. These forms all lost the medial [t] early on, as seen in such spellings as *Crismas* in Middle English, and later dialect use in Scots *Chrissenmas*, Yorkshire *Kessenmas*, and others.

The combined forms are there from the outset: *Christmas Day* in Old English; *Christmas Eve* and *Even* in Middle English; *Christmastide* and *-time* from the end of the sixteenth century. And that's the period when we see recorded for the first time many of the combinations known today: *Christmas carol*, *cake*, *pie* (see *mince pies*, p. 185), *pudding*, *log*, *present*. *Father Christmas* makes his first literary appearance too, in the 1640s, when the Puritans banned Christmas in England, leading to a great deal of Royalist satirical writing. *Christmas* was personified as 'old Father Christmas' in such pamphlets as 'The Arraignment, Conviction and Imprisonment of Christmas'.

The nineteenth century saw the next big growth in *Christmasly* and then *Christmassy* expressions: *crackers*, *trees*, *decorations*, *cards*, *hampers*, *stockings* are all recorded for the first time. A verb arrived: *to Christmas*, meaning both 'to spend Christmas somewhere' ('We Christmassed in France') and 'to decorate in a Chistmassy way' ('The shops are Christmassing already'). A euphemistic expletive of dismay or exasperation is recorded as the century ended: *Jiminy Christmas!* or *Jiminy cricket!* – used by those who were sensitive about using the name of Jesus Christ as an interjection. It settled down as just *Christmas!* in the twentieth century, along with other slang expressions, all of uncertain origin, but carrying the tone of children's coinages: *Crimbo* from the 1920s, *Chrissie/Chrissy* from the 1940s, and *Crimble* in the 1960s.

Since at least the sixteenth century the word had been used for the period surrounding Christmas Day, as in 'Where are you spending Christmas this year?' or folklore songs such as 'The Twelve Days of Christmas'. But idiomatic usage in the twentieth century took it well beyond that. 'Christmas comes but once a year' said the old proverb. Not any more. If something good happens unexpectedly, or you receive a surprise present, 'Christmas has come early', and it could be any time of year. Similarly, 'all my Christmases have come at once', if the fortune is especially good. And festivals held in the summer months in the northern hemisphere have attracted such names as *Christmas in July*.

Finally, unlike any other entry in this book, this name has attracted a widely used abbreviation: *Xmas*. The *X* was used in Anglo-Saxon times as a representation of the first letter of the name of *Christ* in Greek (*kai*). It was used in several words, such as *Xtian* ('Christian'), and it became popular as an abbreviation for *Christmas* after the sixteenth century. It even developed its own pronunciation: [eksmas].

Christmas creep

Insects, animals, plants and people have been described as moving close to the ground, *creeping*, since the earliest Anglo-Saxon times; the word is common to all Germanic languages. But it doesn't seem to have been used to refer to the movement of events and activities until the mid-twentieth century. It then captured the notion that something has received a gradual increase that takes it well beyond its original purpose. The implication is usually that this is a bad thing. If there is a *price creep*, fore example, prices are going up, not down.

The word has come into its own to describe the arrival of a yearly festival at an increasingly earlier time. Any event and season can be affected, the primary factor being commercial: to lengthen the selling interval for seasonal merchandise. I've already noted the effect in the entry on *Halloween* (p. 130). In the case of Christmas, advertising and selling can begin as early as August. Christmas markets open in October or November. We often hear people say they are 'doing Christmas shopping early this year'.

The English missionary poet John Bradburne tried to reclaim the feast day in his tongue-in-cheek poem 'A Goose's Answer to Xmas' (1979):

> Here's to the happy hilarious years
> When nobody ever sent cards
> Or warned you in June you'd be soon in arrears
> For posting for Christmas: ye bards…

His appeal to poets was to remember the event as a holy time.

Christmas creep is especially noticeable in the musical world. A new Christmas pop song might be available in the autumn, or even the summer, in the hope that it will get into the charts in good time. But this domain illustrates an interesting point: early releases are nothing new. Elvis Presley's first Christmas album was released on 15 October 1957. Even earlier, Gene Autry released a record on 6 October 1947. It was called 'Here comes Santa Claus'.

Christmas pudding see ***plum duff***

eggnog

It's chiefly an American drink now, popular in the festive season (including Thanksgiving, p. 140) but its origins are found in medieval Europe, with a different name. A *posset* was a drink made from hot milk mixed with something alcoholic, and with spices or other ingredients to add flavour. It's often referred to in English literature, perhaps most famously in Shakespeare's *Macbeth*, where we read that Lady Macbeth drugs the possets of the grooms guarding King Duncan so that they won't wake up when her husband carries out his murder.

Possets travelled with the early colonists to America, and by the beginning of the nineteenth century they had developed as a new recipe, a new seasonal focus and a new name, *eggnog*, often shortened to *nog*. As the name indicates, it was then being made with an egg mixture – today, purchasable in separate cartons – optionally stirred up with hot beer, spirits or any other alcoholic brew. Its warmth gave it a winter-season appeal, especially at Christmas, and prompted the addition of seasonal spices such as cinnamon, cloves and nutmeg. It was a common belief that it was Santa's favourite drink during his delivery round on Christmas Eve.

Neither *posset* nor *eggnog* have known etymologies. There are all kinds of possible sources for the intriguing *nog* element. In the seventeenth century we see it being used for a strong variety of beer in some parts of England, especially East Anglia. There may be an echo of *grog* (rum). And then there's *noggin*, also with a relevant history. In the sixteenth century it named a small drinking vessel, and soon after the word was applied to the contents, as in 'a noggin of ale'.

Off-topic – but an inevitable question – what about *noggin* as a colloquialism for 'head'? This was originally boxing slang. It has a different etymological line, going back to a use of *nog* in the sixteenth century meaning a piece of wood, especially an important piece, used as a support for something. It fitted nicely into a view of a 'wooden head' – an insult for someone perceived to have little intelligence – seen also in other wood-related metaphors, such as *blockhead* and *thick as two short planks*.

Father Christmas see ***Christmas***

figgy pudding

It's unusual to be able to pinpoint the popularity of a word with precision. It's even more unusual to find that popularity manifesting itself just once a year. But that's what we have here.

Fig arrived in English, a borrowing from French, in the thirteenth century. There's little sign of the derived adjective, *figgy*, until the eighteenth, when it appears in combination with *pudding*. As a recipe, it has everything in common with plum pudding (see *plum duff*, p. 190), but linguistically it seems to have been a more restricted usage, chiefly in the south-west of England. Some called it *figgy duff*.

There was no special link with Christmas in its early years. It was the popularity of a Christmas carol that made it a familiar expression – for most people, just once a year: 'We Wish You a Merry Christmas'. It's thought that this simple greeting had long been part of a traditional tune sung in the west of England, but it wasn't known elsewhere until a Somerset-born music teacher, Arthur Warrell, made an arrangement of it in December 1935 for a madrigal group at Bristol University. Just the pronoun has altered from his original version, which was *I Wish You...* When it was published, it was called 'A Merry Christmas: West Country Traditional Song'.

After the opening verse, and between the choruses, *figgy pudding* dominates, sung three times in each verse.

> Now bring us some figgy pudding,
>   And bring some out here!
>
> For we all like figgy pudding,
>   So bring some out here!
>
> And we won't go until we've got some,
>   So bring some out here!

The allusion is to the way carol singers would go from door to door, expecting treats (or money) as payment, and not leaving until they were provided. The lines are unlikely to have reflected a doorstep reality. Having done a fair bit of carol singing in my time, I don't recall ever receiving anything remotely resembling a figgy pudding.

But that's neither here nor there. By the early 1940s the carol was a regular feature of concerts, often sung at the end as a rousing piece of merrymaking after the more reflective carols. Indeed, in the days when children came round carol-singing, I recall one group knocking on our door and singing this piece. We asked them to do another, but it turned out it was the only one they knew!

Groundhog Day

Another folk custom associated with the 2nd of February, Candlemas Day (p. 159), was to observe the behaviour of hibernating animals to predict seasonal weather: would winter continue or would spring arrive early? Pennsylvanian Dutch settlers brought it from Europe to North America, where they applied it to the emergence of a local rodent, the groundhog (a member of the squirrel family), from its burrow. According to the folklore, if it's frightened by the sight of its shadow on *Groundhog Day*, it will go back into its burrow, which means there are more winter weeks to come.

The earliest known citation for the name is 1865, with inverted commas around it, and with lower-case initial letters. And that's where the linguistic story would have ended, if it hadn't named a film: a hugely successful fantasy romantic comedy made in 1993, which reinforced the use of capital letters and made the expression known worldwide.

It also introduced a new idiom. The film is about a cynical, unsociable television weatherman, played by Bill Murray, who wakes up one morning and finds he is in a time loop, having to live a day of his life repeatedly until he changes his ways. The notion evidently resonated with the viewing public, for within a year people were applying it to situations and periods which they felt were monotonous or lacking in variation. It proved to be a convenient way of describing their experience of unnecessarily repeated behaviour, boring daily routines, pointless movie remakes, endless repeats of radio or television programmes and cliché-ridden political speeches. 'This feels like Groundhog Day!'

first footing

This New Year custom is found mainly in Scotland, Ireland, the Isle of Man and the north of England, though sporadically encountered elsewhere, such as in the English south-west, or spread by immigration. I live in North Wales, and first learned of it from a local family with a Scottish background. The name began as *first foot*, recorded as a noun from the late eighteenth century. People would talk about 'letting the first foot in' or comment that they had 'a lucky first foot'. In the nineteenth century we see it used as a verb: someone would *first-foot* a household. Then usage largely shifted to *first footing*.

The reference is to the first person to enter a house after midnight on New Year's Eve, and whose presence promises good fortune for the householders as long as traditional requirements are met. David Lodge's novel *Deaf Sentence* (2008) tells the story of a deaf professor of linguistics who at one point goes to lip-reading classes. His teacher describes the custom, and Lodge gives one of the best descriptions I've come across:

> The man who crosses the threshold first after midnight must be tall and well built, mustn't be lame or have a squint, must carry a piece of coal, a piece of bread, and a bottle of whisky, but not a knife, must not be flat-footed or have eyebrows that meet in the middle, must not wear black or speak until he has put the bread on the table, the coal on the fire and given the whisky to the head of the house, after which he says 'Happy New Year' and exits by the back door.

The deaf narrator adds:

> It seems that he doesn't have to be able to hear anything said to him, so I would qualify.

All kinds of folklore explanations have been offered for the requirements, which vary quite a bit from place to place. The symbolism of survival and prosperity is a common feature: coal for a fire, something to eat, something to drink, a coin for wealth, salt for preserving food. It's been suggested that some of the criteria – especially the need for the visitor to be a dark-haired man – are folk memories of invasion by fair-haired Vikings, who brought bad times. The belief was deeply held. There are many accounts of households paying someone to make the visit if they couldn't supply the right kind of male themselves.

Is the custom dying out? Not in some places, where the criteria have been relaxed, with female visitors accepted, and any hair colouring (even ginger, which was always especially feared). And there are promising signs of revival. I was especially taken by the report that, in Dundee in 2018, the Lidl supermarket brought in a special stock of coal for first footing. Customers were given a piece at checkout.

Handsel Monday

It's an unfamiliar name outside of Scotland, though it did spread to Ireland and northern England. The word is there in Old English: *hand* (in its usual sense) + a form of the verb *selen*, meaning 'to give, grant'. *Sell* has the same root, but here the reference is to a gift, not anything for sale. In early Scandinavian languages, such as Old Icelandic, a *handsal* was a joining or shaking of hands to confirm a promise or a bargain of some kind.

In English it was used mainly as a noun, and often spelled *hansel*: one would give someone 'a handsel', especially to mark the beginning of something, such as a new job, a new house, or a new year (in the sense of an anniversary or birthday). The tradition is still recognized in house-warming presents, as well as innumerable greetings cards wishing people good luck with a new venture.

That sense of 'fortune, luck' goes back at least to the thirteenth century. One would wish someone 'good hansel' or 'happy hansel', and hope they would have no 'ill hansel'. Later, shopkeepers would use it for the first sale of the day – in the hope of a good selling day ahead. It could also be used ironically: giving someone *a hansel* could be something unwelcome, such as a clip on the ear.

In Scotland, from at least the early seventeenth century, it named the first Monday of the new year. As time went by, it was usually called *Auld* (or *Old*) *Handsel Monday*. It was an occasion when servants and providers of outside services (such as those who delivered newspapers or the mail) would be given a token gift – a reward for services rendered. Children especially appreciated the day. If they had new clothes, a hansel (usually a coin) would be found in the pocket. And a visit to uncles and aunts on Handsel Monday would definitely be worth their while.

hibernal

The word is from Latin *hibernalis* 'wintry', and came to be used in English in the seventeenth century to describe anything 'relating to winter' or 'appearing in winter', and often opposed to *vernal* (p. 80). It had both a literal and figurative use. Writers would talk of *hibernal weather* or *hibernal growth*, in the context of botany or zoology; or describe someone's time of (old) aging as *hibernal* – in the winter of their life, as it were. The word wasn't often used outside of scientific settings.

It's the related forms that have become really well known. *Hibernation* was the earliest, used in the seventeenth century, but not yet for animals. Rather, it described the action of passing the winter somewhere: 'hibernation in Greece will be very nice'. The notion of a winter sleep for certain animals isn't recorded until the 1700s, along with the verb *to hibernate*, and associated vocabulary, usually specialized, such as zoological *hibernaculum*, for an animal's winter quarters.

The figurative sense of hibernating, applied to people, then had something of a renaissance. Ideas, controversies and principles might all be said to *hibernate* if deferred – placed 'on the back burner', as the twentieth-century idiom puts it. Poet Robert Southey, in a prose dialogue with ghostly Thomas More on the state of society, published in 1824, makes a caustic comment about his lethargy:

> Inclination would lead me to hibernate during half the year in this uncomfortable climate of Great Britain, where few men who have tasted the enjoyments of a better would willingly take up their abode.

But not all uses of *hibernal* are so passive. At the opposite extreme there's a race introduced by the International Trail Running Association in February 2025. It's 50 miles around the hills of Hampshire and West Sussex, and includes some 6,500 ft of climbing. They call it *Hibernal Hills 50*. It's difficult to imagine anything further away from a period of lethargy.

hiemal

The word is from Latin *hiems* 'winter', and came into English in the sixteenth century [pronounced hie-mal]. It's one of several alternatives to *wintry*, but it's never had a great deal of use, apart from by poets, who appreciated its soft [m/l] sounds. Nor have its associated words had a long life: *hiemation*, *hiematical*, to *hiemate*. No usage is recorded after the 1700s, though doubtless the occasional instance can be found in specialized texts. This word family seems to have lost out to *hibernal* (p. 173).

However, probably because of its rare usage, *hiemal* has recently appealed to companies and artists looking for an interesting new name. It's named a warm balaclava hoodie, and also a padded long jacket. And it has a presence in the music world, naming songs, an album, and an ambient band – two, in fact: one in New Zealand and the other in France. The artists fully exploit the underlying meaning of the word. In one song titled *Hiemal*, from the Polish metal band Winterforge, the lyrics are all about snow, darkness and barrenness. In another, the French singer known as Atkiak created a solo project in 2017. He explained in an interview: 'Musically, it is winter-themed drone ambient with layers of field recordings, the objective being to create an immersive, cold soundscape.'

Hiems has also been personified, notably by Shakespeare at the end of *Love's Labour's Lost*. He comes on stage, along with Ver (spring, p. 80) and ends the play with two stanzas of farewell reflection.

> When icicles hang by the wall,
> And Dick the shepherd blows his nail,
> And Tom bears logs into the hall,
> And milk comes frozen home in pail,
> When blood is nipped, and ways be foul,
> Then nightly sings the staring owl
> 'Tu-whit
> To-who' – a merry note,
> While greasy Joan doth keel [*cool*] the pot.
>
> When all aloud the wind doth blow,
> And coughing drowns the parson's saw [*wise saying*],
> And birds sit brooding in the snow,
> And Marian's nose looks red and raw,
> When roasted crabs [*apples*] hiss in the bowl,
> Then nightly sings the staring owl
> 'Tu-whit
> To-who' – a merry note,
> While greasy Joan doth keel the pot.

hoar frost see ***Jack frost***

Hogmanay

This is a word that's recorded in a huge number of spellings over the years, the earliest dating from the fifteenth century, but none of them offer a real clue to the etymology. Given the close political links between Scotland and France in the Middle Ages, a popular theory is that the word came into English from French, with the *-manay* element an adaptation of *l'an neuf* 'the new year'. But that doesn't explain the *hog-* part, and various proposals have been made, including sources in Old Norse and the Celtic languages. As the word was originally a shout-out, that first element could reflect an attention-getting interjection – a 'ho' of some kind. A version of Latin *hoc* 'this' is also possible (thus: 'this new year'); that word was sometimes pronounced *hog*, as illustrated by the Welsh schoolteacher Evans in Shakespeare's *The Merry Wives of Windsor*. But these remarks only hint at the many competing theories for the origins of this word.

Its cultural history is clearer. It began as an end-of-year tradition in Scotland and the north of England, chiefly used by children going from door to door on 31 December and calling for a gift – usually something to eat. The custom is summed up in a nineteenth-century rhyme:

> Get up, goodwife, and shake your feathers,
> And dinna [*don't*] think that we are beggars,
> For we are bairns come out to play,
> Get up and gie's [*give us*] our hogmanay.

The dialect spellings and words show how the focus of the tradition was firmly based in Scotland.

By the end of the sixteenth century we see the present-day event taking shape as a celebration during New Year's Eve, institutionalized with a capital *H*. Its lexical scope rapidly grew, as shown by the many adjective combinations using the name, such as *hogmanay cake*, *hogmanay night* and *hogmanay festival* – the latter capturing the way the time frame developed, with celebrations taking place over several days. There's also a greeting: *Happy Hogmanay!* = 'Happy New Year'.

And, of course, there are *hogmanay songs*, chiefly *Auld Lang Syne*, probably Scotland's most famous linguistic export, known and sung worldwide. Most people are aware that *auld* is 'old' and *lang* is 'long'. *Syne* is less easy to interpret: it's a shortened form of Middle English *sythen* 'since'. *Langsyne* is recorded in the sixteenth century with the meaning 'long ago'. So, *for auld lang syne* = 'for old times' sake'.

Jack Frost

This personification of frosty weather is recorded since the eighteenth century. *Jack* was the obvious choice, as it had long (since the 1300s) been used as a succinct way of talking about 'the common man'. It still has that use, as seen in such expressions as *every man jack* or *jack of all trades*. In the sixteenth century it also developed a negative sense: a *jack* could be a rogue or a scoundrel; and it's that suggestion of naughtiness which characterizes the young sprite-like mischief-maker who in the eighteenth century is recorded for the first time as *Jack Frost*. He's often associated with another personification, *Old Man Winter* (p. 148).

Frost (and *freeze*) is a common Germanic word, and – unsurprisingly, for the British climate – is there in the earliest Old English glossaries. It attracted a range of adjectives expressing its severity, such as *hard* and *sharp*, and a few that offered some relief, such as *light*. The adjective *frosty* was an early derivative; and in the following centuries we see a wide range of expressions describing frost-related conditions such as *frostbitten*, *frostnip* and *frosted*. The coinages continued into the twentieth as new freezing technologies developed: *defrost* is probably the most commonly encountered.

Frost words were clear candidates for figurative development, and by the 1600s they were being used to describe a cold or unfriendly manner or temperament. Shakespeare uses *frost* in that way in the final act of *Much Ado About Nothing*, when Don Pedro wonders why Benedick has 'such a February face, / So full of frost, of storm and cloudiness'.

The metaphorical application went in the other direction in the case of *hoar frost*. *Hoar* was another Germanic word, and appears in Old English to describe the white or grey hair and beard of an old man, especially one who was venerable, such as King Hrothgar in the Anglo-Saxon epic poem *Beowulf*. It was a natural extension, then, to describe the feathery white deposit formed by the freezing of dew, and often described as *white frost*.

Kris Kringle

This is one of several variant spellings, all foreign-looking, which must have been part of its appeal when it arrived in American English in the mid-nineteenth century. The first element would have been familiar as the given name of Dutch and German settlers (and is certainly common in American names today). The second sounds like an English *-ingle* word – and indeed there is such a word, *cringle*, describing the protective rim of a hole in a textile or a sail. There's also *crinkle*. Both go back to the sixteenth century, and have had variant spellings with an initial *k*. There's no semantic association with Christmas, though.

For the origin of *Kris Kringle*, I can't do better than quote the succinct summary in H.L. Mencken's classic study, *The American Language* (originally published in 1919; I quote from the abridged text of 1963). In his chapter 4, in a section on the first loanwords in American English, he writes:

> The American *Krisskring'l* or *Kriss-Kringle*, now rare, arose from a misunderstanding of the German *Christkindlein* or *Christkind'l* which means, not St Nicholas, but the Child in the Manger. Kriss Kringle is traced to 1830 and marked an Americanism.

He's referring to *Webster's New International Dictionary*. He adds that 'a German friend tells me that [these forms] are both unknown in Germany'. He might have added: 'or in Britain', though the influence of American writing, films and television has given it a certain presence there now. There's a similar (British) adaptation in *Christingle* (p. 161).

It's not so rare these days. And the name is also known in some other English-speaking countries, such as Canada, the Philippines and Ireland, where it's developed a second use, and sometimes an alternative spelling. A report in the *Irish Independent* in December 2018 explains:

> Secret Santa season, or Kris Kindle as it's traditionally known in Ireland, is in full swing... primarily a Western tradition, and if you've played it before, you know the drill. A group of colleagues, friends or family members are assigned to purchase a Christmas gift for each other anonymously. Names are usually pulled out of a hat and the gift receivers have no idea who their 'secret Santa' is.

The report comments that the latter name is now more common. Indeed it is. But as there are online gift exchange options these days – Kris Kringle generators and other apps – the old name is in no danger of disappearing.

Lucy light

The expression remembers a traditional rhyme, in which St Lucy, a fourth-century Roman martyr, is in contrast with Saint Barnabas (see p. 93), 'Barnaby bright'. She's the patron saint of the blind. But the combination of *Lucy* and *light* is an etymological tautology, as both words relate to Latin *lucidus*, 'shining', and belong to the same semantic family as *lucid*, *lucent*, *lux* and other words to do with light and illumination.

Her feast day is 13 December, which in the Old Style calendar was the winter solstice (p. 30), the shortest day. In Anglo-Saxon times that day was considered to be of special importance, a reason for a holiday, and she came to be given a prime liturgical status, one of the few female saints mentioned by name in the traditional Canon of the Roman Catholic Mass. Although the day later diminished as a public festival in England, its significance was not forgotten by poets. John Donne was one, in the early seventeenth century capturing the essence of the shortest day in the opening lines of 'A Nocturnal upon St Lucy's Day':

> 'Tis the year's midnight, and it is the day's,
> Lucy's, who scarce seven hours herself unmasks;
> The sun is spent, and now his flasks
> Send forth light squibs, no constant rays...

In some other countries her name is by no means forgotten. The festival of *Sankta Lucia* is especially popular in Sweden, with candle-lit processions and other events.

And *Lucy Lights* is well known in Zurich, where since 2010 it's named the Christmas display along the city's main shopping street, Bahnhofstrasse. The saint is only an indirect allusion, though, as the origin is the Beatles' song 'Lucy in the Sky with Diamonds'.

Martinmas

This is the feast day of the fourth-century saint Martin of Tours (in central France), 11 November, and celebrated in many parts of Europe with fairs, bonfires, candlelit processions and other festivities. Looking back, it marked the end of the harvest season; looking forward, the beginning of winter. It developed a special status as a quarter day in parts of England and Scotland – a day when servants would be hired, school terms started, leases terminated and rents paid (*Martin rent*). The name is recorded in English from the fourteenth century, along with various uses as an adjective, such as *Martinmas Day* and *Martinmas Eve* (for the evening before), and describing the kinds of food traditionally eaten on the day, notably *Martinmas goose* and *Martinmas meat* (beef).

Martinmas competed with expressions in which the saint is named separately, as in *St Martin's Eve*, and also with phonetically simplified forms, as the sequence of [n] + [m] evidently presented a pronunciation difficulty. We see *Martymes* in the fifteenth century, for example.

But the form that became widespread in the sixteenth was *Martlemas*. Shakespeare uses it figuratively in *Henry IV Part 2*, when Poins asks Bardolph, 'And how doth the Martlemas your master?' He's referring to the portly Falstaff, aware that the feast day was one associated with plentiful food.

There was a popular association with the weather. In the seventeenth century we see any period of mild sunny weather around the feast day being called *St Martin's summer*, and later *Martinmas summer* (see also p. 134). Thomas Hardy was another who saw the figurative potential in the name. In *The Mayor of Casterbridge* (1886) he describes a new time for the newly married wife of the mayor:

> A Martinmas summer of Mrs. Henchard's life set in with her entry into her husband's large house and respectable social orbit; and it was as bright as such summers well can be.

It must be the repeated [m]s in the name that has given it a certain appeal to twentieth-century writers. Plot lines have revolved around *Martinmas murders*, *mysteries* and *magic*. Indeed, expect to see it combine with any atmospheric *m*-word that offers an alliterative punch, such as *midnight* and *miracle*. Maybe even *Microsoft*.

mince pies

Originally these were simply pies containing minced meat – a usage still found in Scotland, and brought by Scottish settlers to New Zealand. The adjective is from the verb *mince*, which came into English from French in the fourteenth century, meaning 'to cut up food into small pieces'. By the seventeenth it had developed a figurative sense: '*anything* cut up into small pieces' – hence the idiom *to make minced meat of* someone, later spelled *mince-meat*, and today usually *mincemeat*.

Meanwhile, a secondary sense developed – a mixture of currants, spices and other ingredients baked in pastry – and by the time of its first recorded use in 1604 it was already associated with the season of Christmas. In a New Year letter to Stella in 1710, Jonathan Swift sends a cheeky rhyme:

> I wish you both a merry New Year,
> Roast beef, minced pies, and good strong beer,
> And me a share of your good cheer,
> That I was there, or you were here;
> And you're a little saucy dear.

The following year, in another letter, he spells it *mince pies*, and that became the norm, often hyphenated.

That would seem to be the end of the linguistic history of *mince pies*, until the mid-nineteenth century, when it was picked up by the Cockney fraternity as rhyming slang for 'eyes' – almost always in the plural. James Joyce in *Ulysses* praises someone for having 'a prime pair of mincepies'.

Then, as often happens in rhyming slang, it shortened to *minces* or *mincers*. 'Keep your minces open!' As with so many rhyming expressions, it's unclear just how much present-day use there is, but evidently enough for it to head an online Christmas recipe in 2016: 'I can't believe my minces!'

mistletoe

The name is found in the first Old English glossaries, *mistle* being common to the Germanic languages as the name of a white-berried plant that grows on the branches of some trees. The second element is etymologically interesting. It was originally *tan* [pronounced tahn], the Old English word for a shoot growing from a tree or bush. But the plural of the word for a toe, *ta* [tah] sounded the same: *tan*. The two words became confused.

By the end of the Anglo-Saxon period, the *tree*-related word had fallen out of use (to be replaced by *twig*), and the *-n* ending of the *toe*-word was also disappearing (to be replaced by *s*, *toes*). 'Mistle-twig' thus became 'mistle-toe' – though the old *-n* wasn't forgotten, recorded even as late as the seventeenth century. It's there in two of the three forms listed in Thomas Blount's dictionary of hard words (1659), *Glosographia*: *Messelto*, *Meseldine*, *Misteiden*. And in some English dialects, such as those in and around East Anglia, the *-n* is remembered in a variety of spellings even into the twentieth century, such as *misselden*, *mislin* and *mizzlin*.

The plant was credited with magical and medicinal powers in many European folk traditions, especially when (unusually) growing on an oak tree. Its evergreen leaves and its blooming in winter led people to see it as a symbol of fertility, vitality and love, as well as a form of protection against evil powers. In England it came to be associated with Christmas as a popular decoration, and by the eighteenth century the custom had arrived of kissing under the mistletoe as a sign of love, whether already in place or being hoped for.

As with many old traditions, it has been thought that mistletoe had lost its magic with the younger generation, and that the kissing custom was dying out. But popular culture seems to have ensured its survival. Justin Bieber had a Christmas album in 2011, which he called *Under the Mistletoe*, and the plant named its catchy lead single, with its lead word repeated in every verse.

And then, as if that wasn't enough to give the word a new lease of life, Harry Potter goes and does the same thing, in *Harry Potter and the Order of the Phoneix*. There's mistletoe in the mysterious Room of Requirement in Hogwart's Castle, and that's where Harry and fellow witch-student Cho Chang share a first kiss. Even if others forget the mistletoe tradition, Potterheads will keep it alive.

nival

It's a borrowing from Latin *nivalis*, meaning 'snowy', with a first recorded use in the seventeenth century, but it never became frequent until it was adopted in the nineteenth for specialized use in such fields as physical geography, zoology, ecology and earth science. A region of perpetual snow would also be described as *nival*, and the region just below it (or under it) as *subnival* or *subniveal*.

A small cluster of derived forms appeared. If the ground around or under a snowbank melted to leave a shallow depression in the ground, the process came to be called *nivation*. There was also *nivosity*, referring to anything that resembled snow. *Niveous*, another seventeenth-century coinage, achieved a wider range of use, some writers finding it an impressive alternative to *snowy*.

Nival appealed to companies involved in providing protection against wintry conditions – *Nivalsport*, for example, produces a wide range of outdoor and sports items, such as clothes for skiing and snowboarding, rainwear and windbreakers. I've also found it in a few artistic settings where the creator wants a wintery appearance, such as a brand of wallpaper.

But beware! Some of the commonest cultural uses have nothing to do with snow, as when we see it naming a software development firm, a brand of jewellery or a strategy video game. In Ireland it's the acronym for the National Irish Visual Arts Library. And then, as far away from winter as it's possible to imagine, it names a boutique hotel on the Mediterranean Greek island of Sifnos.

Plough Sunday, Plough Monday

In England these were two days, recorded since the fifteenth century, but certainly much older, that marked the start of the ploughing season. They formed the first agricultural festival of the year, beginning on the Sunday after the feast of the Epiphany on 6 January. On that day the village plough would be decorated and brought to the local church to be blessed. There would be a service praying for a good harvest, and a procession with a special candle, the *plough light*. Afterwards, there would be a *plough feast*, with a special *plough pudding*, and much revelry. The festival would continue into the Monday. As one eighteenth-century writer described it:

> On this day the young men yoke themselves, and draw a plough about with music, and one or two persons, in antic dresses, like jack-puddings, go from house to house, to gather money to drink.

The festival largely died out at the Reformation, but was revived in Victorian times, and is still recognized in some rural areas, especially in the north of England. As farms became larger and mechanized, a symbolic tractor, or part of a traditional plough (such as the ploughshare), would be brought to the church.

Unsurprisingly, given its central role in agriculture, *plough* became the source of a large semantic family, with over two hundred expressions recorded since Anglo-Saxon times for types of plough, the parts of a plough and its uses (such as *plough-furrow*). Curiously, the name of the actual vehicle isn't recorded until the fourteenth century, but the word *ploh* is there in Old English in the sense of 'plough-land', and beginning in the 1300s we see the growth of the associated vocabulary, with *ploughman* and *ploughswain* (for the farmers) and *ploughwright* (for the makers). New technology brought more coinages, such as *snowplough* in the eighteenth century.

One interesting linguistic development affected the spelling. The word is recorded in a remarkable number of variant forms in the Middle Ages (*plogh*, *plouh*, *plowhe*...), but by the eighteenth century it had settled down as *plough*, with the final consonant silent in all but a few regional accents in the north of England and Scotland, where it continued to be sounded as [f] or [ch] (as in *loch*). It was fixed in British English when Dr Johnson included it and its associated forms in his *Dictionary* of 1755. But the variation didn't go away, as a few decades later lexicographer Noah Webster made it one of his simplifications for American English: *plow*.

plum duff

Plum is Germanic in origin, and found in Old English. So is *duff*, but in its original form, *dough*. The history of the *gh* spelling in English is complex, becoming silent in such words as *thought* and *through*, but sounded as [f] in others, such as *rough* and *enough*. *Dough* is unusual in that it went both ways: the *gh* kept its silence in standard English; but in some northern dialects of England, and also Scotland, it was re-spelled, following local pronunciation, as *duff*.

It begins to appear in written records for a kind of boiled pudding, cooked in a *duff bag*, and containing currants or other sweet ingredients, including plums (when it was called a *plum pudding*). It seems to have been popular with sailors, judging by the contrast drawn by an anonymous US Navy officer, writing in the New York monthly magazine *The Knickerbocker*, in 1838. He describes several wonderful treats produced by the ship's cook, Mr Tudor, and then becomes ecstatic:

> And oh! – that 'duff' – that *plum* duff! – plum-pudding, as land-lubbers would have awkwardly called it – of a Sunday!

Its maritime association with Christmas can be seen in Richard Henry Dana's memoir *Two Years Before the Mast* (1840). In chapter 4 he gives us a convenient description:

> To enhance the value of the Sabbath to the crew, they are allowed on that day a pudding, or, as it is called, a 'duff'. This is nothing more than flour boiled with water, and eaten with molasses. It is very heavy, dark, and clammy, yet it is looked upon as a luxury, and really forms an agreeable variety with salt beef and pork.

Then, in chapter 8, he reports:

> Thursday, Dec. 25th. This day was Christmas, but it brought us no holiday. The only change was that we had a 'plum duff' for dinner, and the crew quarrelled with the

> steward because he did not give us our usual allowance of molasses to eat with it. He thought the plums would be a substitute for the molasses, but we were not to be cheated out of our rights in this way.

It's left the sea long behind today, but kept its link to Christmas: there are online recipes for plum duff still (on the BBC Food website, for example). But the name has lost out to *Christmas pudding*, along with its medieval folklore – made with thirteen ingredients representing Christ and the twelve apostles; stirring it from east to west to remember the journey of the Magi in that direction; and including an inedible treasure (such as a silver coin) to be found by one of the eaters. Many families still have a stirring ritual; but money discoveries are rare in an increasingly cashless age.

posset see ***eggnog***

Santa Claus

It's still possible to hear the phonetic origin of this name in *Saint Nicholas*, especially if it's said quickly, dropping the medial *o*. In the fourth century he was Bishop of Myra, a Roman town in the south-west of what is now Turkey. His Christmas fame stems from his reputation for generosity, with several stories of his secret gift-giving to the poor – notably, in one legend, putting gifts in the shoes of children, left outside their homes at Christmas-time for that purpose, and often exchanged for a morsel of food provided for his horses.

The name first appears in English in the eighteenth century, having been brought to New Amsterdam (now New York City) by Dutch settlers, for whom the name was *Sinterklaas*, showing the same phonetic shortening. Its first recorded use in the *New York Gazette* in 1773 shows a curious spelling, *St. A Claus*, which may well have influenced the form that by the twentieth century had become the elliptical standard, *Santa*.

This personification of Christmas is so familiar nowadays that it needs no recapitulation here. Nor is there much to be said linguistically, other than to note the various combinations that have used his name, such as *secret Santa* (see p. 181). There have also been some clever coinages associated with the children's custom of sending him a letter – or, these days, an email – to his traditional address at the North Pole. My favourite is the one used by the Canadian post office: Santa's postal code is HoH oHo.

secret Santa see ***Kris Kringle***

snow

It's not surprising, given the northern climate, to find the noun *snow* in all the Germanic languages, and present in the earliest Old English writings. It has since generated a huge semantic family, with over 300 members. *Snow-white* is one of the earliest, along with *snowy*; in Middle English we find another adjective, *snowish*, and the verb *to snow* in the fourteenth century. *Snowdrift* and *snowball* are among the newcomers in the fifteenth, followed by a huge range of coinages in the sixteenth, such as *snow-time*, *snow-bright*, and *snow-cold*.

The following century continued the lexical growth (*snow-covered*, *snow-like*, *snowdrop*, *snowshoe*...). *Snowflake* arrives in the eighteenth, along with *snowstorm* and *snowplough*, as well as several descriptive adjectives such as *snow-capped* and *snow-mantled*. And lexical creativity has continued ever since, with *snowfall* and *snowman*, *snow-flurry*, *snow-scape* and over 150 more in the nineteenth – a remarkable century for vocabulary in this field – then into the twentieth with *snow-globe* (the toy), *snowmobile*, *snowbuggy*, *snow tyres*, and more. Spelling usage varies: spaced, hyphenated or solid?

Many of these coinages soon developed figurative senses and idioms. *Snowball*, for example, expressing the notion of increasing in size, is recorded in the seventeenth century, and then the evocative *snowball's chance in hell*, in American English in the 1930s, later shortened: 'you haven't a snowball's chance of getting there'. It got even shorter in the 2000s: 'I don't give a snowball's about that.' It's not often that we see a possessive ending being used in this way.

Snowflake has had an unusual metaphorical history. It's been applied to people since the 1980s, and was originally quite positive, drawing on the notion that no two

snowflakes are alike to describe a person's uniqueness. But in the early 2000s it somehow developed a negative sense, and became a term of mockery for anyone considered to be easily offended or being unreasonable in demanding special treatment. It's surprising to see a word switching its meaning so dramatically in such a short time.

sugar plum

The name can mislead, as *plum* isn't being used here in its sense of fruit. What has happened is that the smallness and roundness of a plum has been taken over to describe other edibles. In the mid-seventeenth century it named dried grapes or raisins used in cakes and puddings, as in *plum pudding* (p. 191). And in the same period we see *sugar plum* naming a small round or oval colourful confections made of hard boiled sugar, and containing various flavouring ingredients such as nuts or dried fruit.

Sugar plums could make their appearance at any time of the year. In 1709 Joseph Addison writes in the *Tatler* of an occasion where he was invited to dinner, and included in dessert were 'little plates of sugar-plumbs, disposed like so many heaps of hail-stones'. The date was 21 March. But everything changed during the nineteenth century, after Clement Clarke Moore wrote *'Twas the Night Before Christmas*:

> The children were nestled all snug in their beds
> While visions of sugar-plums danced in their heads.

The association was reinforced when Tchaikovsky composed his music for the ballet *The Nutcracker*. It tells the story of a little girl who travels to the Land of Sweets on Christmas Eve. One of the characters she meets is the Sugar-Plum Fairy, whose dance has become one of the most popular pieces.

It's a quirk of historical lexicography that a figurative sense of *sugar-plum* is actually recorded earlier than the literal sense. Anything that was very pleasant might be called a sugar plum, especially when something was being given as a bribe. The earliest recorded use is by dramatist Thomas Dekker, who published a pamphlet in 1609, *Lanthorne & Candle-light*, about 'villainies discovered by candlelight' in London. One of his characters is a prostitute who sweet-talks a suspicious officer 'by stopping the Constable's mouth with sugar-plums (that's to say), whilst she poisons him with sweet words'.

The expression has since had a wide appeal. Apart from the many online recipes, I've found it naming a boutique in Fleet, a tea room in Ruthin, brands of gin and chocolate, and several plant species. And one American blogger addresses her readership as *sugarplums*. It would have been *sweeties* in the old days.

wassail

The word isn't recorded in English until around 1200, but its origin in Old Norse *vess heill*, meaning 'be healthy', suggests that it was brought in by the Danish settlers in eastern England during Anglo-Saxon times. The phrase was used as a salutation, said when presenting a bowl of liquor to someone, or when passing it around a table, much as we say 'good health' or 'cheers' today. The expression could be heard at any time of the year, but came to be strongly associated with the Christmas season.

Wassail soon developed a range of uses as a single word. It began to refer to the bowl or the liquor it contained: a servant might enter carrying *a wassail*. The drink was typically a strong spiced ale, judging by the alliterative expression *wine and wassail*. Shakespeare uses it in *Macbeth*, when Lady Macbeth plans to make King Duncan's grooms drunk with 'wine and wassail'. And in *Hamlet* King Claudius is said to 'keep wassail' – riotous festivity. The seventeenth century also named the people who kept wassail: *wassailers*.

Even more common was the use of *wassail* as a verb, also recorded in the thirteenth century. People would sit around *wassailing* – drinking and revelling. And as the association with Christmas celebrations developed, some would *go wassailing* around a neighbourhood – or, as the nineteenth-century carol says:

> Here we come a-wassailing
> Among the leaves so green;
> Here we come a-wand'ring
> So fair to be seen.

A later verse makes it clear who's involved:

> We are not daily beggars
> That beg from door to door;
> But we are neighbours' children,
> Whom you have seen before.

During the seventeenth century we see several expressions finally recorded for the first time, such as *wassail cups*, *wassail bowls* and *wassail candles*. And that century is when we find references to a local custom of visiting fruit trees or livestock early in January, to wish them good health for the forthcoming year. A visit on or around Twelfth Night and the feast of the Epiphany (6 January) was especially favoured. And while the practice of going to orchards appeared to have been dying out in the twentieth century, it seems to have had a renaissance in the twenty-first, especially in places where there's a history of cider production. For example, the Barley Wood cider company has held an annual community wassail event in Somerset for several years. By all accounts, it's a sell-out.

winter hedge

This expression never entered standard English, but it had a lively time in several regional dialects of England, especially Yorkshire, Lancashire and Derbyshire, and also in Scotland. Standard English in the nineteenth century would know it as a *clothes horse*. But during the previous century we see *winter hedge* reflecting an everyday country practice.

Clothes would traditionally be laid out on a hedge or bush to dry, air and bleach; but when winter came this was often not possible. As a result, people devised hinged upright frames that could be placed on the floor indoors, or racks suspended from the ceiling, on which they could hang their laundry, and used a *hedge* analogy to name it. Any such contraption could also be called a *clothes hedge*. There was also a dialect use of *dyke*, usually a word that named prominent channels or dams, but sometimes fences and hedges, and so: *winter dyke*.

Then, one of the strangest seasonal usages in this book, describing a metal rack hung by a source of warmth, such as the bars of a fire grate, which could hold a kettle, iron or other kitchen implement. It was called, simply, a *winter*.

Joseph Wright in his *English Dialect Dictionary* (1906) found it used across all of northern England in the nineteenth century. He quotes a description of a ruined house: 'The fireplace still stands with its three broken ribs and the old winter in front of them.'

winter of discontent

The words open Shakespeare's play *Richard III*. Richard steps forward to tell his audience about himself, and draws a contrast between the new reign of Edward IV (a 'son of York') and the turmoil of the preceding years of civil war:

> Now is the winter of our discontent
> Made glorious summer by this sun of York.

The expression evidently caught the popular imagination, as it was picked up by other writers in the seventeenth century, and stayed in the language, often contrasted with a previous contented summer. Both seasons could be used figuratively, as with Richard, to refer to a period of time longer than a single season.

In Britain the expression achieved a special resonance in the winter of 1978–9, when widespread strikes occurred, especially after it was used by Larry Lamb in an editorial in the *Sun* newspaper in May 1979. This was a crisis for the Labour Party. Since then, any period of political or industrial unrest is likely to attract the phrase in the media, regardless of the party in power. 'Boris Johnson must beware of new winter of discontent' ran another *Sun* headline in September 2021. And, in the same month, the *New European* asserted: 'Britain enters its Brexit Winter of Discontent'.

It's no longer just winter that causes problems. The other seasons have all been affected. 'Is the UK facing a summer of discontent?' asked the *Guardian* in July 2022, and followed it up in September 2024 with 'Keir Starmer's autumn of discontent'. And then, 'Are we looking at a spring of discontent?' opened an article in *The Spectator* in April 2025.

Even shorter periods can be so described. Choose your month: 'a — of discontent'. 'UK business heading for a January of discontent' headlined a piece in the *Financial Times* in December 2024. *Cycling News* in 2005 reported some poor competition performance by two cyclists, heading the piece 'A July of discontent'. Sports writers seem to love it. A bad series of match results can shorten the period further, as in this headline from the *Guardian* in March 2025: 'Arsenal moving on up after a week of discontent'.

I thought a week would be the lowest limit for the expression, but no. Planning a protest next Wednesday? Someone is sure to call it 'a day of discontent'.

winter woollies

Wool is a common Germanic word, found in the earliest Old English texts. Curiously, the adjective *woolly* isn't recorded until the end of the sixteenth century, and the noun *woolly* not until the mid-nineteenth. It described any garment or covering (such as a blanket) made of wool, or a combination of garments for the whole body, and was thus usually found in the plural: *woollies*. The British climate soon made *winter woollies* its most frequent use.

It was the First World War that gave the expression a major boost. This was a time when women all over the country were asked to knit socks, balaclavas, scarves and other warm items for the troops abroad. The website of the Wool Company summarizes:

> Women across the country formed knitting clubs in towns and villages. Social norms relaxed to allow knitting on buses, in queues, at shops, theatres, dinner parties, and even between courses at restaurants. It was even said that the Archbishop of Canterbury decreed that people were allowed to knit during sermons.

There was a jocular use too, with music-hall comedians often asking their audience if they 'had their winter woollies on'.

The wartime effort continued into the Second World War, and letters from the time show how much these gifts were appreciated. A writer in the February 1940 issue of *The Wire* (the magazine of the Royal Corps of Signals) reports that 'the men have found their … winter "woollies" sound protection against winter winds'. It's interesting that he felt it necessary to add inverted commas, presumably worried about using such a colloquial expression in print.

If I thought the expression was in danger of dying out, I was reassured by the band who call themselves the Bar-Steward Sons of Val Doonican. They play folk instruments and sing cleverly satirical pieces, giving comedic lyrics to well-known songs. They name themselves as the missing children of the popular Irish singer who usually appeared wearing knitted jumpers. They too wear brightly coloured knitted tank-tops as a tribute to their 'father'. (A linguistic note: Bar-Stewards was chosen as a friendly euphemism for Bastards.) They called their 2024 tour *Winter Woollies*.

If that isn't enough to guarantee future use, you'll find the expression naming a range of soft cuddly animal toys as well as a selection of Christmas cards with a woollen jumper motif. And we mustn't forget the advice of the Consumer Council for Water, which ran a piece in 2012 asking 'Have your water pipes got their winter woollies on?'

Xmas see ***Christmas***

Yule

In Germanic languages it named a winter festival, and this was carried into Old English, where it came to be used both for Christmas day (*yule-day*) and for the surrounding season. The month of December was sometimes called 'before yule' and January 'after yule' (see also Appendix, p. 225).

During the Middle Ages it became widely used as an adjective. In the fourteenth century we see the night before Christmas being called *yule-night*, in the following century *yule-even*, and then in the sixteenth *yule-tide* was used for the season as a whole. By that time *Yule* was beginning to be printed with a capital *Y* (or *U*, when spelled *Ule*). In the seventeenth century we see *Yule-cakes*, *Yule songs* (carols) and *Yule-games*. The *Yule log* (also called a *Yule block* or *Yule clog*) became an important tradition, especially in Scotland and the north of England – a large bough of a tree, ceremoniously brought into the house, often carved with protective symbols, and kept burning for the twelve days of the season.

A linguistic novelty (along with *April Fool!* and *Christmas!* pp. 42, 162) is its use as an interjection – a joyful exclamation shouted as people left a church service. It's first recorded in the sixteenth century, but doubtless the practice long predates it. Lexicographer Thomas Blount explains it, in one of the longest entries in his dictionary *Glossographia* (1659), spelling it *Ule, Yeule* and *Yool*. He ends his entry with a description:

> In Yorkshire & our other Northern parts, they have an old custom, after Sermon or Service on Christmas day, the people will, even in the Churches cry *Ule, Ule*, as a token of rejoicing, and the common people run about the streets singing
>
> Ule, Ule, Ule,
> Three puddings in a Pule,
> Crack nuts and cry Ule.

I hope this book will sometimes be dipped into during the Christmas season, but even if it isn't, I trust readers will forgive me if I nonetheless end this section with that old shout.

Yule! Yule!

winter sayings

- Winter's thunder makes old man's wonder.
- Winter eats that summer gets.
- Winter fills the ponds before it freezes them.
- Every mile is two in winter.
- One kind word can warm three winter months.
- A green winter makes a fat churchyard.
- Bad wintering will tame both man and beast.
- An early winter,
  A surly winter.

After winter followeth green May.
GEOFFREY CHAUCER, *Troilus and Criseyde*

SEASON CONTRASTS

Winter is cold-hearted,
Spring is yea and nay,
Autumn is a weathercock
Blown every way:
Summer days for me
When every leaf is on its tree.

Christina Rossetti, opening stanza of 'Summer', 1881

Sing a song of seasons!
Something bright in all!
Flowers in the summer,
Fires in the fall!

Robert Louis Stevenson, final stanza of 'Autumn Fires', 1885

Autumn to winter, winter into spring,
Spring into summer, summer into fall, –
So rolls the changing year, and so we change;
Motion so swift, we know not that we move.

Dinah Maria Craik, opening lines of 'Immutable', 1854

The entries in the previous four sections have explored the way words relating to the individual seasons have influenced the English language; but often the focus is more on the contrast between them, or on what happens when unexpected seasonal events blur their traditional boundaries.

The linguistic consequences are most obvious when new words are coined by blending two months from different seasons, or by adding an unusual adjective or noun to a month ending. The practice has sometimes prompted a social media craze, with dozens of idiosyncratic celebratory creations such as *Veganuary*, *Fabruary* (LGBTQIA+), *Marchintosh* (classic Macintosh computers), *Jawgust* (the film *Jaws*) and *Dogtober* (dog rescue campaigning). Some have achieved a status within particular communities, such as *Gaypril*, prominent especially among US universities as an occasion for LGBTQIA+ celebration.

But being playful with month names has a much longer history. Anthony Burgess was a fan. Taking his cue from James Joyce, he provides an example in his account of Joycean linguistic creativity, *Joysprick* (1973), imagining a drunkard punbaptising the months of the year:

> Ginyouvery, Pubyoumerry, Parch, Grapeswill, Tray, Juinp, Droolie, Sawdust, Siptumber, Actsober, Newwinebar, Descendbeer

A short selection of monthly blend names and seasonal contrasts provides a fitting conclusion to the theme of this book.

blends

Here are five of the seasonal portmanteaux (as Lewis Carroll would call them) created in recent times.

Augtober

This can work both ways: the weather in August can feel like October, or October can feel like August. But the word has had a broader appeal. Some fashion firms have used it as an eye-catching moment outside the usual fashion seasons (see p. 213) – for example, Prairy Sky Jewelry Co. has an Augtober Collection. The name also identifies an instance of 'holiday creep', when a yearly festival begins to be celebrated well ahead of its time (p. 165). Here it's Halloween that's anticipated, with shops selling pumpkins, scary decorations and other topical goods. As one website headlined: 'Augtober. It's officially spooky season now.'

Croptober

This is a seasonal agricultural coinage with a difference. It became widely recognized in the early 2000s to describe the main harvest season for those in the northern hemisphere cultivating cannabis outdoors. October is the turning point of the year for the plant, following a summertime when there's (usually) plenty of light and warmth, and preceding a period when temperatures begin to fall.

It's not known who invented the nickname; it seems to have emerged informally among growers, especially in places where legal constraints on cultivation were relaxed. It was then adopted enthusiastically by the cannabis-using community, who saw it as a special time for evaluating the year's fruitfulness, and an opportunity to share techniques and technology about the growth cycle of the plant in its various strains. Cannabis harvest festivals now provide an occasion for celebration, and a forum to discuss economic, legal and other cultural issues.

Drycember

This coinage started out in northern climes as wordplay for an unusually rain-free winter month. *Dryvember* expressed the same notion. But it wasn't long before other connotations of *dry* pushed these words in new directions. In December 2020, a Texan culinary enthusiast, Darcy Baldwin, used *Drycember* for an online series of YouTube videos about food dehydration for preservation. But the main new use captured the intention of going alcohol-free for a month. Several people have used *Dryvember* as a charity fund-raising opportunity. Some students have decided to have a *Drycember* to ensure better end-of-year exam or assignment grades. However, people are pragmatic, and if they decide to give up alcohol for December they tend to stop on the 23rd. As one online proponent put it: 'It's a pre-emptive strike against the evils of overindulgence.'

Juneuary

This is another two-way seasonal coinage, also spelled *Junuary*, that became popular in the northern hemisphere, especially in British Columbia and north-west USA, during the later decades of the nineteenth century. Said in June, it relates to cool, rainy, wintery weather. Said in January, it's unexpectedly warm and sunny. Needless to say, it's the former period that tends to attract most attention.

In recent years, the name has travelled beyond North America. A UK headline in the *Telegraph* in June 2024 referred to one of the issues:

> 'My husband is insisting on 22 degrees': The central heating wars erupting in dismal 'Junuary'.

The strapline read: 'Telegraph staff share their tips for keeping the peace during this year's gloomy summer'. I hope they worked.

Movember

This is a global charity that hosts an annual event in November with the aim of raising awareness about men's health issues. It encourages clean-shaven men to grow moustaches ('mo's') throughout the month to draw attention to the campaign and to foster donations to the Movember Foundation. The name motivates a great deal of wordplay. Men who participate are 'Mo-Bros', and women who help are 'Mo-Sisters'. People are encouraged to 'mo' ('move') with activities like walking and running, and to 'host a mo-ment' – an event to raise awareness and funds.

Snowtober

A coinage for the unseasonable arrival of snow in a region where, in the northern hemisphere, it's two months early. *Snowvember* is another, when it's one month early. And there have even been autumnal *Snowtembers*, such as in Calgary, Alberta, in 2014. The southern hemisphere has also found that a useful blend: there was a spring *Snowtember* in South Africa in 2024.

When in October 2011 a snowfall happened across the Canadian maritime provinces and north-eastern US states, there was a media debate over what to call it. Should it be *Snowtober*, *Octsnowber*, *Snoctober*, *Shocktober*, *Oktoberblast*...? *Snowtober* won, presumably because the retained long vowel of *snow* made the meaning transparent. And since 2011 it's been the name of choice whenever snow falls in that month.

contrasts

Writers, and especially poets, love to compare and contrast the seasons. Often it's a literal reflection about the changes in weather, proverbial in its succinctness, and – as is common with proverbs – sometimes offering contradictory advice:

> Winter's thunder is summer's wonder.
> Winter thunder bodes summer hunger.

The American poet James Russell Lowell brings spring and winter together in the acerbic opening lines of 'May is a pious fraud' (from *Under the Willows and Other Poems*, 1869):

> May is a pious fraud of the almanac
> A ghastly parody of real Spring
> Shaped out of snow and breathed with eastern wind;
> Or if, o'er-confident, she trust the date,
> And, with her handful of anemones,
> Herself as shivery, steal into the sun,
> The season need but turn his hour-glass round,
> And Winter suddenly, like a crazy Lear,
> Reels back, and brings the dead May in his arms.

Probably the shortest ever contrast between a month and a season comes from Scottish comedian Billy Connolly:

> there are two seasons in Scotland:
> June and Winter.

age

The most widespread practice is to see the seasonal contrasts as a metaphor of aging. Summer versus winter has always been the main focus. We see them neatly juxtaposed in *The Passionate Pilgrim*, a collection of twenty poems published in 1599 with Shakespeare's name on the title page (though not all are by him). Poem 12 includes these lines:

> Youth like summer morn, Age like winter weather;
> Youth like summer brave, Age like winter bare.

A contemporary of Shakespeare, writer Richard Greene, brings a metaphorical spring into contrast with autumn in the opening story of his *Mourning Garment* (1590). He paints a picture of an unbelievably handsome youth, Sophonos, who 'in his tender years carried grave thoughts, and in the spring of his youth, such ripe fruits as are found in the autumn of age'.

The associated months are often used to identify age differences. Chaucer, in his *Merchant's Tal*e, describes the marriage of a rich old man to a young wife: their names are January and May. December later came to replace January, and 'May–December affairs' became a common expression.

Another of Shakespeare's contemporaries, playwright Thomas Dekker, wrote of Cruelty in the last chapter of his book *The Seven Deadly Sins of London* (1606). That sin included forcing young girls to marry rich old men; he harangues his readers:

> will you be careless in coupling your Children? into whose bosom threescore winters have thrust their frozen fingers, if he be rich ... you dishonour Age.

and he sums it up:

> you do wrong to Time, enforcing May to embrace December.

September sometimes intervenes, allowing an extra stage in the relationship. A popular modern instance is the piece Kurt Weill wrote for the 1938 Broadway musical *Knickerbocker Holiday*, 'September Song'. It sounds like another May–December affair, as an old man is trying to persuade a young woman to be his wife. But he thinks of his age as only September, and promises that he'll be faithful in the following months until he reaches December, which is now his death month:

> But it's a long, long while
> From May to December
> And the days grow short
> When you reach September.

Frank Sinatra picked up the message when he included the song in a studio album in 1965, when he was 50. He called the album 'The September of My Years'.

living

The various moods, events and opportunities of everyday life provide another domain of seasonal comparison. Any proposal or plan can evoke the proverb 'If you do not sow in the spring you will not reap in the autumn.' And Berowne in Shakespeare's *Love's Labour's Lost* expresses his commonsensical approach to life:

At Christmas I no more desire a rose
Than wish a snow in May's new-fangled shows,
But like of each thing that in season grows.

The arrival of news attracts the metaphor too: summer news is joyful and pleasant; winter news is the opposite. Other Shakespeare examples: Innogen in *Cymbeline* asks her servant Pisanio what's in a letter that he's bringing to her. She suspects the worse from his face:

If't be summer news,
Smile to't before; if winterly, thou need'st
But keep that count'nance still.

And in *Henry VI Part 2* the Duke of Gloucester awaits the passing-by of his banished wife:

Thus sometimes hath the brightest day a cloud;
And after summer evermore succeeds
Barren winter, with his wrathful nipping cold;
So cares and joys abound, as seasons fleet.

love

The growth of love, with all its successes and failures, has also attracted season contrast metaphors. There's an obvious parallel between changes in nature and changes in a relationship, and many poets and lyricists have explored it. Themes such as these recur:

- the beginning of romance, the excitement of falling in love – *spring*
- greater intimacy, warmth, passion, sharing experiences – *summer*
- challenges to be addressed, opportunities for soul searching – *autumn*
- a relationship cooling, perhaps ending, or deepening into a new vision – *winter*

Jonathan Larson wrote a song for the 1996 Broadway musical *Rent*. He called it 'Seasons of Love'.

An early poetic instance occurs in Lady Mary Wroth's *Urania* (1621), the first romantic novel written by an English woman. She makes seasonal references throughout, and at the end of her story there's a sonnet sequence, which includes a 'song' in which all four seasons are named. Here are the opening two quatrains:

> The Spring time of my first loving,
> Finds yet no winter of removing;
> Nor frosts to make my hopes decrease:
> But with the Summer still increase.
> The trees may teach us Love's remaining,
> Who suffer change with little paining:
> Though Winter make their leaves decrease,
> Yet with the Summer they increase.

In the pronunciation of the time, *removing* and *loving* would have rhymed, each having the short vowel of *love*.

transitions

It's not common to see compound nouns in which two seasons are joined with a hyphen or slash mark, but it does happen. All four possible combinations are found. *Winter–spring*, for example, has a first recorded use of 1888; it's used when something takes place during both seasons, or in the transitional period between them. The world of fashion especially uses this sort of expression, with *spring/summer* and *autumn/winter* (or *fall/winter*) collections (p. 13).

There's also a technical medical term, recorded since 1898, identifying a malarial fever that can occur in late summer in temperate regions. Its Latin origins are reflected in the name: *aestivo-autumnal* (*estivo-autumnal* in American English), from *aestivus* 'summer' and *autumnalis*. It's unlikely to be encountered outside of medical journals.

Can there be compounds that skip a season? *Autumn–spring* has been recorded since the seventeenth century, describing a period of warm spring-like weather occurring in the autumn. It even developed a figurative sense, meaning a late period of growth (as with an *Indian summer*, p. 134). We see it used in this way by writer Thomas Forde, an apprentice of the Stationers' Company who became an author, known for his celebration of the restoration of Charles II in 1661, *Virtus Redivivi* ('Virtue Reborn'). This was subtitled *A panegyrick on His Sacred Majesties most happy return*. It includes a dialogue between two lords, discussing how the new king will find a wife. One lord has an interesting reversal of the May–December theme:

The fire of love hath thaw'd his frozen breast,
And turn'd his cold *December* into *May:*

His colleague replies:

Love can create an Autumn Spring, infuse
New spirits in the old, and make them young.

It evidently happened – though 'old' hardly applies in this case. The 'merry monarch' married Catherine of Braganza in 1662, when he was 32.

APPENDIX

month stories

People who know the Latin numerals for 7, 8, 9, 10 – *septem*, *octo*, *novem*, *decem* – can be puzzled by the fact that the month names *September*, *October*, *November*, *December* don't match up, running not from 7 to 10 but from 9 to 12. The explanation lies deep in Roman history.

The story begins with the original Roman year, associated with the legendary Romulus, the first king of Rome, which had only ten months. The tradition states that he named the first month of the year *Martius*, after his father Mars, the Roman god of war. Several festivals of Mars took place in this month, probably in anticipation of war campaigns later in the year.

Goddesses are thought to be reflected in April, May and June: *Aprilis*, possibly from Aphrodite, the goddess of love and procreation; May from *Maia*, the eldest of the seven sister nymphs, the Pleiades, associated with growth and fertility; June from *Juno*, associated chiefly with marriage.

After those four months, imagination seems to have run out. The remaining months were simply given numerical names: the fifth, sixth, seventh, eighth, ninth and tenth months – *Quintilis*, *Sextilis*, and then the familiar *September*, *October*, *November* and *December*

The ten-month year became twelve, according to tradition, during the reign of the second king of Rome, Numa Pompilius. January and February were added at the beginning of the year. *Januarius* is from another deity, *Janus*, the doorkeeper of heaven, and thus the guardian of the year-opening. February is from *Februarius*, which in turn is from *februa*, referring to the various practices of purification used in and around the festival of Lupercalia on the 15th (from the god Lupercus – the Roman equivalent of the Greek god Pan). The surprising thing is that the names of the later months were left unchanged, hence the legacy seen in September, etc. above.

We're now two months away from the modern calendar. July appeared when *Quintilis* was renamed *Julius* in 44 BCE to honour Julius Caesar because it was the month of his birth. August was named a few decades later, in 8 BCE, to honour Augustus Caesar, the founder of the Roman Empire, whose successful campaigns often culminated in that month.

extensions

All these names are recorded in Anglo-Saxon times, and some of them became a prolific source of English vocabulary. A natural development was to name plants and insects whose growth or appearance is associated with a particular month. So we find at various times *March violet*, *May lily* and *June apple*, *February red* (a type of stonefly), *June beetle* and *December moth* – and dozens more. Nearly a hundred expressions are listed in the *OED* for May, many to do with the outdoor celebrations that take place during that month (see p. 60). Curiously, hardly any are recorded for July and August.

Adjectival coinages formed with a suffix are recorded from the seventeenth century. The usual ones are *-like* (*April-like, May-like, June-like*) and *-ish*, which became popular in the eighteenth century (*Aprilish, Novemberish, Decemberish* and, later, *Septemberish*). Probably all the months have been used with these suffixes in everyday speech, though not formally recorded by lexicographers. There have been some less usual suffixes noted too: *Septembrian*, *Novembery* and *Decemberly*. For some reason April has attracted more coinages than any other month: *Aprilian* in the seventeenth century and *Aprilesque* in the nineteenth. It's also given rise to two of the most widely used expressions, which have separate entries in this book: *April fool* (p. 43) and *April showers* (p. 42).

It would seem unlikely to have month names used as verbs, but there are some instances. The oldest and commonest is *May*, recorded since the fifteenth century to mean 'take part in May day or May month celebrations'. In the nineteenth century we see a writer saying how he 'Novembered and Decembered at the Park'. There are several examples of an American colloquialism, *to June* or *June around*, meaning 'to hurry, wander about', or (as one writer defined it) 'to be busy but not accomplish anything'. And in the same century we see a single instance of *august* meaning 'ripen, bring to fruition'. It occurs in the middle of Philip James Bailey's long narrative poem 'The Mystic' (1855):

> He for the cause of the dear nations toiled,
> And augusted man's heavenly hopes.

There have also been a few literary metaphorical adaptations. In Shakespeare's *Much Ado about Nothing,* Don Pedro asks Benedick why he looks so serious (see also p. 179):

> What's the matter?
> That you have such a February face.

And in the same play he has Don John describe young Claudio as 'a very forward March-chick'. The expression presumably has a literal source, for a chicken hatched in that month; but here it describes a precocious or presumptuous youth.

Probably the most famous literary use is in Lewis Carroll's *Alice's Adventures in Wonderland* (1865): *March hare*. The excitable behaviour of male hares during their breeding season, when they leap about and chase around in circles, was noticed as early as the fifteenth century.

People would talk about being 'as brainless, merry or mad as a March hare', and it's the madness motif that became proverbial.

This section would be incomplete without a mention of *Juneteenth*, or *Juneteenth Day*, the American name for the holiday on 19 June commemorating the emancipation of African-American slaves in Texas on that date in 1865. And I end with a speech curiosity: the modern pronunciation of *July* has the stress on the second syllable, but until the late eighteenth century it was always on the first – echoing the stress pattern of *Julius*. Read this line from the sixteenth-century poet Edmund Spenser's *The Faerie Queene*, and the metre clearly indicates the stress: 'Then came hot July boiling *like* to fire.'

an Anglo-Saxon footnote

What were the months called in English before the Roman names arrived? The eighth-century scholar–monk Bede gives us a convenient listing in his popular work *De temporum ratione* ('Of the reckoning of time' – see also my entry on *Easter*, p. 45). The symbols *Ð*, *ð* and *þ* were all pronounced 'th', and the *g* of *geol* as in 'yule'.

January *Æftera-geol-monaþ* – 'after the month of Yule'.
February *Solmonaþ* – 'sun-month' (acknowledging the return of the sun) – but the name has also been interpreted as 'month of cakes', the allusion being to ritual offerings of cakes and loaves to hope for a good harvest.

March *Hreðmonaþ* – 'month of Hreða' (a Germanic goddess associated with fertility, glory, victory).

April *Eosturmonaþ* – 'month of Eostur or Eostre' (a Germanic goddess of the dawn), whose festival was close to the spring equinox; a predecessor of Easter.

May *Đrimilce-monaþ* – 'month of three milkings' (well-fed cows, from new spring grass, allowing them to be milked three times a day).

June & July *Liþa-monaþ* – 'travelling month' (from a verb meaning 'travel', though there may be a link to *liþe* 'mild, gentle, pleasant'. To distinguish them, June was also known as *Ærra-liða-monaþ* ('first, former') and July was *Æftera-liða-monaþ* ('second, later').

August *Weod-monaþ* – 'weed-month' – some things don't change.

September *Haligmonaþ* – 'holy month' (when religious festivals would be held after harvest).

October *Winter-fylleð* – 'winter full moon' (winter began with the October full moon).

November *Blotmonaþ* – 'blood sacrifice month' (the killing of livestock to hope for a mild winter).

December *Ærra-geol-monaþ* – 'month before Yule'.

moon names

English has accumulated a wide array of folklore names for the full moon of each month, many inherited from Native American, Germanic and Celtic cultures. They typically reflect local weather conditions in the northern hemisphere, or seasonal plant and animal activities. This is just a selection; several names have variant forms due to differences in translation.

January	Ice Moon, Moon after Yule, Quiet Moon, Severe Moon, Stay Home Moon, Wolf Moon
February	Bear Moon, Hunger Moon, Ice Moon, Snow Moon, Storm Moon
March	Chaste Moon (from the purity of the spring season), Sap Moon, Worm Moon (from earthworm trails)
April	Egg Moon, Fish Moon, Easter (or Paschal) Moon, Pink Moon (after local wildflowers)
May	Flower Moon, Hare Moon, Milk Moon
June	Berries Ripen Moon, Green Corn Moon, Horse Moon, Hot Moon, Mead Moon, Planting Moon, Rose Moon, Strawberry Moon
July	Buck Moon (from the regrowing of antlers), Hay Moon, Thunder Moon
August	Fruit Moon, Grain Moon, Sturgeon Moon

September	Barley Moon, Full Corn Moon, Harvest Moon, Song Moon, Wine Moon
October	Blood Moon (from sacrifices made), Drying Rice Moon, Falling Leaves Moon, Hunter's Moon, Michaelmas Moon, Seed Fall Moon, Travel Moon
November	Beaver Moon, Darkest Depths Moon, Frost Moon, Freezing Moon, Mourning Moon
December	Cold Moon, Long Night Moon, Moon before Yule

Easter egg solutions (from p. 49)

In the *Easter* entry:

- 'I've wondered about it a hundred times.' Said by Harry Lime's girlfriend, Anna Schmidt, when talking to Holly Martins about Harry's supposed fatal accident.

In the *Easter egg* entry:

- 'Be seeing you.' The regular expression of farewell used by the inhabitants of the Village to each other.

REFERENCES

I make several references to Joseph Wright's *English Dialect Dictionary*, compiled singlehandedly over a decade and self-published in 1906. An equally dedicated team at the University of Innsbruck have made it available online: www.uibk.ac.at/en/disc/blog/english-dialect-dictionary-online. Also online is the unabridged *Oxford English Dictionary*, www.oed.com, an unequalled source for historical lexical usage.

I use a few longer modern quotations. The extract from the poetry of Lord Kilian in the *spring roll* entry can be seen online at https://allpoetry.com/Lord_Kilian. The extract from the poetry of John Bradburne in the *Christmas creep* entry is also online at www.johnbradburnepoems.com, and selections of his poetry (edited by me) are available through the John Bradburne Memorial Society: www.johnbradburne.com.

The quotation from H.L. Mancken in the *Kris Kringle* entry is from his multi-volume study *The American Language*, first published in 1919 by Alfred A Knopf. I quote from the abridged fourth edition of 1963, published by Routledge & Kegan Paul. Also in that entry is a quote from an article in the *Irish Independent* for 6 December 2018, 'Secret Santa traditions from around the world', available in its archive at www.independent.ie/storyplus/secret-santa-traditions-from-around-the-world/37601439.html.

The quotation from David Lodge in the *first footing* entry is in chapter 17 of his novel, *Deaf Sentence*, published by Penguin in 2008.

The quotation from Allan Metcalf in the *guy* entry is in chapter 9 of his *The Life of Guy*, published by Oxford University Press in 2019. Its subtitle explains: *Guy Fawkes, the Gunpowder Plot, and the Unlikely History of an Indispensable Word.*

PICTURE CREDITS

All the illustrations in this book are wood engravings by Eric Ravilious, which originally appeared in the following publications in the Bodleian Library collection:

Martin Armstrong, *Fifty-four Conceits: A Collection of Epigrams and Epitaphs Serious and Comic*, 1933. Bodleian Library, 28001 f.1002: p. 3

Nicholas Breton, *The Twelve Moneths*, 1927. Bodleian Library, Rec. e.268: pp. 50, 91, 97, 137, 205

Robert Harling, *Notes on the Wood Engravings of Eric Ravilious*, 1946. Bodleian Library, 1712 e.10: pp. 41, 123, 149, 195, 207

Ambrose Heath, *The Country Life Cookery Book*, 1937. Bodleian Library, 1781 e.967: pp. 37, 99, 129, 131

The Wood Engravings of Eric Ravilious, 1972, Lion and Unicorn Press. Bodleian Library, 171 b.67: pp. 4, 6, 9, 11, 31, 35, 38, 44, 79, 85, 87, 88, 116, 119, 120, 143, 145, 146, 208

INDEX

OF WORDS & PHRASES

INDEX

OF PERSONS

GENERAL

INDEX